Created for Responsibility

Created for Responsibility

by Tony Headley

EMETH PRESS
www.emethpress.com

Created for Responsibility

Library of Congress Cataloging-in-Publication Data

Headley, Anthony J.
  Created for responsibility / Anthony J. Headley.
    pages cm
  Includes bibliographical references.
  ISBN 978-1-60947-094-4 (alk. paper)
  1. Christian ethics. 2. Responsibility--Religious aspects--Christianity. I. Title.
  BJ1251.H34 2015
  241--dc23
                        2015022314

To

Adina, Jon, Aaron, Alex and Melissa

Table of Contents

Chapter One

Created for Responsibility

T hen God said, "Let us make man in our image, after our likeness; and let them have dominion over the fish of the sea, and over the birds of the air, and over the cattle, and over all the earth, and over every creeping thing that creeps upon the earth." So God created man in his own image, in the image of God he created him; male and female he created them. And God blessed them, and God said to them, *"Be fruitful and multiply, and fill the earth and subdue it; and have dominion over the fish of the sea and over the birds of the air and over every living thing that moves upon the earth"* (Genesis 1:26–28, italics mine).

Stories of Irresponsibility, Old and Modern

From the dawn of creation, God's been calling us to respond to his claims on our lives. He's been trying hard to make us responsible. But, as if in some cosmic game of

to respond, our lives are built on responsibility to God

"pin the tail on the donkey," we keep running from responsibility. Adam and Eve set the pace. That much appears abundantly clear in the Genesis account of the Fall:

> And they heard the sound of the LORD God walking in
> the garden in the cool of the day, and the man and
> his wife hid themselves from the presence of the LORD
> God among the trees of the garden. But the LORD God
> called to the man, and said to him, "Where are you?"
> And he said, "I heard the sound of thee in the gar-
> den, and I was afraid, because I was naked; and I hid
> myself." He said, "Who told you that you were na-
> ked? Have you eaten of the tree of which I com-
> manded you not to eat?" *The man said, "The woman
> whom thou gavest to be with me, she gave me fruit
> of the tree, and I ate."* Then the LORD God said to the
> woman, "What is this that you have done?" *The
> woman said, "The serpent beguiled me, and I ate"*
> (Genesis 3:8–13, italics mine).

The exchange sounds like a classic case of passing the
buck, the kind one expects in a case of "whodunit." This
is the stuff of children caught red-handed. "I didn't do it!
He did!" "No, I didn't, she did." Nobody takes responsibility for anything. Certainly, not Adam and Eve! Instead,
they passed the buck. Adam blamed Eve. Eve blamed the
serpent. Adam, in a twisted kind of reasoning, pointed
his finger at God. After all, if God hadn't given him the
woman, he wouldn't be in all this mess. At least, that's
how he sought to justify himself.

We have followed this same pattern ever since. Examples like Adam and Eve's abound. Like them, we frequently blame others for our sinful choices and actions.
I found two good examples in *News of the Weird*. The
fact that I read news like this may say something about
me. But the stories are true. Most just have strange twists
to them.

The first story involved Anthony P. Clemente. He was on trial in a Boston court for the murder of four rival gang members. However, he refused to accept responsibility for the murders. Instead, with an Adam-like twist, he blamed the police. He said: "You [the police] should have stopped [the feud] a long time ago. You guys got snitches. You should know what's going on. The [police] department's partly responsible."[1]

In the same edition, a similar story appeared. Wendell Williamson had been convicted of a 1995 shooting rampage in Chapel Hill, North Carolina. In that rampage, he killed two people. In June 1997, he filed a lawsuit against psychiatrist Myron Liptzin. Dr. Liptzin had treated him in the spring of 1994 for paranoid schizophrenia. In the lawsuit Williamson accused the psychiatrist of being the real culprit. Why did he make such an accusation? Williamson claimed Dr. Liptzin's retirement had pushed him to the rampage; being left without the benefit of therapy, he could not help committing his crime. According to his logic, the psychiatrist was really to blame. During the trial, he was asked whether Dr. Liptzin should be blamed. In all earnestness, Williamson replied: "He had more control over the situation than I did."[2]

Blaming others for their misdeeds makes perfect sense to persons like Anthony Clemente and Wendell Williamson. Ironically, in September 1998, a jury ruled in Williamson's favor. The jury ordered Dr. Liptzin to pay Williamson $500,000. The jury felt Williamson did not understand his illness and expectations and therefore could not be held responsible. Of course, many were outraged. The family of the victims felt Williamson had been rewarded for murder. Bruce Berger, the defense attorney for Dr. Liptzin, said, "At some point, people need to take responsibility for their own actions. This responsibility shifting, which I think is what the jury

did, is wrong." Though I recognize some self-interest in
the defense attorney's statement, at the core, Berger was
right.

We have gone so far in responsibility shifting that
persons now bring lawsuits against fast-food restaurants
for making them fat. They ignore their role in choosing
to buy fattening food in the first place. Sometime ago, I
saw a cartoon that poked fun at this blame-shifting stance.
In the cartoon, a mother brings her grossly overweight
son to an attorney. She tells the attorney that she wishes
to sue the fast food company for making her child fat.
After a pause, the attorney asks, "And who will you sue
for making him ugly?" Not the kindest thing to say! However, it points to the absurd ends that are possible when
persons frivolously shift blame to others for their behaviors and problems.

At other times, we avoid personal responsibility altogether. A sad illustration of this appeared in a local
newspaper story involving teenager Amanda Jo
Amburgey.[3] For most of her 17 years, Bufford McIntosh
had denied being her father. He twice disowned her before legal authorities. Even after a genetic test in 1989
proved his paternity beyond any doubt, he still disowned
her. After a six year delay, the paternity trial was set for
February 28, 1995. McIntosh didn't show. The case was
finally decided on September 27, 1995. The court confirmed his paternity and assessed him $275 per month
in child support.

He didn't pay. By February 1996, he was $2,919 in
arrears. On May 23, 1996, the day before Amanda's tragic
death in a car accident, McIntosh returned to court. This
time he faced contempt charges for nonpayment of child
support. He indicated he had no means to pay. Kim
Jacobs, Amanda's mother, relented; she would forget the
money if he acknowledged being Amanda's father. McIn-

tosh looked Amanda squarely in the eye and said, "You are not my daughter." Amanda died the next day having never heard her father acknowledge her.

I can't think of a worse example. McIntosh sounds like the classic "deadbeat dad." But it gets worse. A wrongful death suit was subsequently filed on Amanda's behalf. Now McIntosh, the same man who denied her for 17 years, seeks half the proceeds from the wrongful death suit. McIntosh now says, "I just want this to be over, to go on with my life and to do what is right by my daughter." Talk about a turnaround!

Defining Responsibility

So far I have used the term *responsibility* to mean owning up to one's choices and behaviors. That's certainly the case in most of the stories illustrated. It's true of Adam and Eve, Clemente, and Williamson. Most of us probably use the word in this sense. But the word also includes the idea of an obligation one owes. That's true in McIntosh's case.

Sometimes I used the term in this latter sense with my teenage sons. For a few years I occasionally reminded my oldest son, "With privilege comes responsibility!" I usually said it when he asked: "But, Dad, why do I have to have to do these chores? Why can't my brothers do them?" Of course, his brothers also had chores. He objected to what he perceived as more difficult jobs. "Well," I would say, "you get a bigger allowance, and you have a few more privileges. When you are ready to trade in your bigger allowance for your brothers' you can be responsible for less." He never wanted to do that. After a while he had my line about responsibility down pat; often, he didn't let me finish. I would begin, "Son, with privilege . . . ." He would quickly chime in, "Yeah, Dad, I know.

With privilege comes responsibility." That's usually all it took for him to get the point. Basically, I reminded him of certain obligations that go along with his privileges and status as eldest son.

I have told that little story to say this: There's much more to responsibility than we sometimes believe. Most of us probably have an intuitive sense of what it means, but we may not know its related features. Just so we are all on the same page, permit me to elaborate.

Responding Appropriately

Sometime ago, I told one of my colleagues about writing this book. He immediately remarked, "Here's a definition for you. Responsibility is the ability to respond appropriately, with wisdom, to various situations." I don't know if this was original or borrowed, but he was right. Responsibility does involve a response. You may readily notice that responsibility derives from a combination of response and ability. That's no accident. When we show responsibility, we always respond to someone or something. When I tell one of my sons to do his chores, I am responding both to him and to a given situation. I may respond that I had found compelling evidence in his room that he had not cleaned it for some time.

My colleague's definition also states that responsibility involves appropriateness and wisdom. Those two pieces are critical. For example, let's suppose I found my son's room pretty messy. I could respond to him and his room in several ways. I could close the door, vowing never to return. Some people actually do that. While conducting a stress management seminar, one woman indicated that this was her strategy. She would simply close the door when her son's room got messy. She figured he would finally get sick of his own mess. Somehow though,

the typical teenager seems to possess a rather high tolerance for mess and clutter.

Having somewhat less tolerance than a teenager, I
could pursue a second alternative. I could clean the room
for him. Thereby I could make an invaluable contribution
to his future wife's woes. Third, I could yell and scream all
over the place and tremendously wound him. All of these
would be responses, but would not be appropriate or wise.
Most of us would likely consider them irresponsible because they lack wisdom and appropriateness.

Responding to God's Claims

What determines appropriateness or wisdom? Should
those judgments be left to our own whims? Or should we
decide by our shifting cultural standards? Obviously, we
need definitive standards that permit judgments about
what is wise or appropriate. We must use some guide-
lines. If we do not have such firm criteria, even foolish
things could be considered wise and appropriate. That's
because we would have no standards but our own. By
these subjective standards, anything could be considered
responsible. The most detestable actions could become
responsible behaviors, at least in the eyes of the one doing the action. No wonder noted theologian Dietrich
Bonhoeffer wrote ". . . responsibility is the total and realistic response of men to the claim of God and of our
neighbor."[4] These claims of God and neighbor provide
the basis for responding wisely and appropriately.

The order is important. God's claims must have priority. Following his claims first rarely leads to harming
our neighbor. In fact, doing so serves our neighbor's well-
being. It's then that we are truly being responsible. We
are acting in light of ultimate reality. Irresponsibility fundamentally involves living as though God had no claims

on us. It is to act as though we could ignore our neighbors' lives and well-being. It is to live as though we alone mattered.

Sometimes, irresponsibility also involves following "neighbor" claims without due regard to God's. For instance, several Nazi leaders followed Hitler in exterminating millions of Jews. In their minds, they acted responsibly since they followed orders. In God's eyes and the world's, this was a heinous crime, the epitome of criminal irresponsibility. Whenever we follow others' directions that contradict God's laws, we act irresponsibly. Only when we act in accordance with God's claims do we truly live responsibly.

There's good reason to believe that ignoring God and his claims is the grand illusion. When we ignore God we inevitably find ourselves living out fantasies. A bumper sticker I saw recently echoes my point. The bumper sticker read: "I have given up looking for truth. Right now I'm just looking for a good fantasy." Is there any other possibility when we ignore God's truth? Ignoring ultimate reality leaves us with nothing but fantasized living.

Why's that? It's because God's laws stand as the highest standards for human responsibility and conduct. They form the true basis for reality. His laws reflect life as it was created to be. Therefore, to follow God's way is to follow reality. To fail to act according to his ways means losing contact with reality. It means living an illusion and a lie. In contrast, to live by God's law is reality-based living at its best.[5] We often discover too late that we have been living an illusion instead of reality.

Living a Lie

Adam and Eve partly lived this illusion by acting as if God's law didn't matter. The serpent's voice and advice mattered more. By following the serpent, they disobeyed God and brought eternal harm upon themselves and their offspring. It wasn't that they didn't know his law. They knew it only too well. Eve and Adam chose to ignore God's law and God's reality. God had forbidden them to eat of the fruit. He told them what would happen if they did—they would die. That was reality. Instead, they ignored his truth and believed the serpent's lie. The serpent basically questioned God's truth: "Did God really say you would die? That's rubbish! You won't die and God knows it. He really wants to keep you from being like him." Believing the lie, they followed the serpent's fantasy. Too late did they discover that God spoke the true reality. They died spiritually; they would die physically. They did not become more like God. They became less like him and less of themselves. Too many persons still trade God's reality for the world's illusions. The consequences remain just as severe.

Responsibility and Relationships

By now, you have probably discovered something else about responsibility; it always involves relationships. As a father, I ought to expect responsible actions from my sons because of our relationship. Always behind responsibility one finds relationships. That's true whether one thinks about relating to people, things or situations.[6]

We see these different relationships in the Genesis account of creation. Adam and Eve bore responsibility to God. They were his creatures and owed him their allegiance. They also carried explicit, God-given responsibility to the created world. No wonder their fall affected them as well as creation. Adam and Eve were also bonded to each other in every sense of the word. As one flesh, they were linked physically. But their bonds also extended to their spiritual and social lives.

No relationship long survives without trust. This reveals something else about responsibility. It cannot exist without fidelity and trustworthiness. When these elements characterize relationships, responsibility is possible. Without them, it's impossible. It would even be considered foolhardy to expect responsible behavior from persons lacking these traits. On the other hand, expecting responsibility from persons possessing these characteristics makes perfect sense. We can rely on them to exercise their responsibilities faithfully. Such persons never lightly ignore or violate their relational obligations.[7] That's why we characterize behaviors such as stealing and marital infidelity as irresponsible. These behaviors violate sacred relational bonds.

Accountability is yet another word related to both relationships and responsibility. To live accountably means acknowledging obligations to others. These obligations derive from commitments we make and the roles we play (for example, the role of spouse).[8] Basically, all obligations involve relationships. Living responsibly means that we must both accept and faithfully live out our relational obligations.

To our credit, we are seeing a renewed emphasis on accountability in our society. This emphasis may indicate a renewed interest in living responsibly. As a result, many churches are forming and using accountability groups. These groups have relevance for all Christians. Responsibility groups can be formed for those desiring a richer Christian life. However, such clusters are especially necessary where there has been a failure at responsibility. Thus one tends to find accountability focused around addictive behavior such as alcoholism. In these gatherings, members make commitments to each other to live Christian lives. They also vow to live above the addictive behavior. The group becomes a means of strengthening resolve and reinforcing behavior, and usually becomes a place of confession and restoration when failure occurs.

Bonded Yet Free

As indicated, accountability assumes relationship. It implies mutual bonds forged with God and others. Such bonds require a new way of living and accountability to our relationships. We see this clearly in Adam and Eve. They were bonded to God as his creatures. Given this relationship, they were to live in fellowship with him. He had laid claims upon them that required obedience. Likewise, Adam and Eve were integrally linked to each other. This meant that they should live in harmony and seek each other's well-being.

But though bound to God and each other, they yet possessed freedom. They were free to choose whether they would respond to God and each other. Freedom to choose was a gracious gift from God's hand. It was not arbitrary but by design and the chosen method for producing responsible lives. God would not force them. Neither would he leave them with no other choice but to obey. They must choose to obey of their own free will.

Some may look at the conditions and wonder whether God set them up for failure. Why did he allow them choice knowing they could choose the wrong? Why didn't he make them do the right thing? The answer appears rather simple; *they could become responsible only if they exercised choice.* Without freedom they could not live responsibly. Freedom and relationships are the linchpins of responsibility. Thus, Dietrich Bonhoeffer emphasized "Without these bonds and without this freedom, there is no responsibility."[9] He's absolutely right. Because of his relationship with us, God calls us to live responsibly. But we must always be free. Without freedom, we are but slaves, servilely responding to the dictates of overlords. Such a strategy would never produce the responsible people God created us to be.

Every parent knows responsibility demands freedom. That's why wise, caring parents give their children more choices as they mature. The only way to raise responsible adults is to give children increasing responsibility as they grow. A parent does so by allowing the child choices, even when the parent would not make the same choices. Of course, I do not mean allowing them sinful choices. I mean allowing children preferences that differ from our own.

Even better than parents, God knows responsibility demands freedom. That's why he made Adam and Eve free. That's why he gave them free will and choice. Not to ensure their failure, but to invite them to grow. Living responsibly was the only way they could become what God intended. Without it, they would remain stunted, mere shadows of their real selves.

"You Are Not Responsible for Everything!"

Because responsibility involves freedom and choice, we must always seek to determine our obligations. We must routinely ask: "What is my responsibility in this situation?"[10] That question implies something else about responsibility; namely that we're not obligated to everything. If we were, we would never need to ask that question or sort through options. Our obligations would be clear. We would respond without thinking and without decision—like so many automatons.

Unfortunately, some Christians frequently act as though they are responsible for everything. They live as if everything depended on them. Thereby they assume responsibility for things not rightfully theirs. They take over other people's lives and obligations. All the while, they believe they are exemplifying essential Christian behavior.

Over-responsible behavior sometimes springs from a misunderstanding of Christian responsibility. Often one finds other influences than Christian belief at work. In the counseling room I have heard a variety of reasons having little to do with being Christian. I mention three reasons here as examples. First, over-responsible behavior often derives from bondage to a script from the past. Some authority figure gave the over-responsible person inappropriate messages about responsibility. Often these persons were "parentified"; they were in some manner asked to take on adult responsibilities far too early. Second, this style often represents a futile attempt to experience a sense of worth and meaning. The latter is mistakenly associated with the number of deeds accomplished or the number of people saved. Third, I have at times found an adolescent, egocentric tinge to this way of being and acting. These persons see themselves as the center of the universe and act as though everything depended upon them. In this one might detect a proud, god-like illusion instead of humble servanthood. That is, the over-responsible person may act as God, endeavoring to be an amateur providence in the lives of others. Sometimes there is a combination of all three reasons in one over-responsible person.

Kathy was one of these over-responsible people. She was a forty-something visiting student whom I met in a marriage and family counseling summer course. I don't remember what led to the conversation. But somewhere in the class, Kathy told us about her problem. In short, Kathy's problem was her sister, Kim. Kim was like a magnet for trouble. She bounced checks, repeatedly lost jobs, drank heavily and navigated occasional brushes with the law. Whenever Kim messed up, she turned to Kathy. Dutifully, Kathy would bail Kim out one more time. Each time, she promised herself and Kim that this was the last time. It never was.

By the time I met Kathy, Kim was in her mid-thirties. She was still getting into trouble and still expecting Kathy to bail her out. Kathy dutifully obliged. From her story, Kathy was obviously becoming weary in her perceived well-doing. She knew something wasn't right. She knew helping Kim didn't really help. Kim simply became more irresponsible. But Kathy couldn't let go of carrying the responsibility for her sister's life and actions. Somewhere in the back of her mind a lingering parental message remained: "Always take care of your baby sister." The trouble was that her sister was no longer a baby, only an extremely childish 35-year-old woman.

Kathy needed to know that God never intended us to assume responsibility for every error and misdeed done by others, even for those we love dearly. He intended us to live responsibly with ourselves and co-responsibly with our neighbor.[11] *Co-responsibility* means our neighbors must carry the greater weight for their own lives. We come along to help with the loads that they cannot manage by themselves. That's part of the reason for our constantly having to discriminate between legitimate and illegitimate responsibility. Oftentimes, our obligations will vary. It is not our responsibility to bail out the Kims of the world. They must carry their own loads if they desire to mature. Sometimes simply praying is the most responsible and loving response.

Making Responsible Choices

But how do we know what our responsibilities are? To discover this, we must be self-aware. We must know what *we* think. Another way to speak about this is to talk of boundaries; that is, having a distinct sense of self that clearly demarcates, or sets off, one individual from another.[12] It means knowing what pertains to me and what rightfully belongs to others. Appropriate decisions derive from such considerations.[13] In short, to relate appropriately with others, we must know ourselves. Without this capacity, we will emotionally overreact rather than act responsibly.

People who do not know what they think, feel, say or want usually live irresponsibly. They usually lack differentiation. They repeatedly confuse themselves with others, failing to distinguish themselves from others. Because they do not know themselves, they tend to act in one of two ways. They may ignore their appropriate responsibilities altogether. They live like Bufford McIntosh, who fathers children but does not claim or support them. On the other hand, others who lack self-awareness go to the opposite extreme. Like Kathy, they may become overly responsible for other people. In the process, they dehumanize others by not expecting them to live responsibly. They also inappropriately overload themselves with others' burdens.

We must also have realistic standards. I have already emphasized that these standards must find their source in God. Without God's standards, meaningful responsibility is oftentimes fictional. For example, an employee may lie to cover his superior's mistakes. In so doing, he may think that he is doing the right thing. However, such behavior is irresponsible. It violates the guilty individual as well as the victims. We get a clearer picture if we recall the Watergate scandal. Several high-ranking officials apparently lied to cover for Nixon. In so doing, they did an injustice to the whole country and they paid a price for their behaviors. By God's and the nation's standards, they acted irresponsibly. Yet, by their standards, they acted responsibly. That's why we <u>must constantly base responsible behavior on God's standards, not on our own private rules.</u> *[handwritten: base responsibility on God's standards, not ours or the worlds]*

Endnotes

1. Chuck Shepherd, "Blame the Police," News of the Weird, *Lexington Herald-Leader*, November 7, 1997.

2. Chuck Shepherd, "Crazy Accusation," Ibid.

3. Judy Jones, "Father by Default," Ibid., November 1, 1997.

4. Dietrich Bonhoeffer, "The Structure of Responsible Life," in *On Being Responsible,* ed. James M. Gustafson and James T. Laney (New York: Harper and Row, 1968), 58.

5. See Bernard Haring and H. Richard Niebuhr, Ibid. Both acknowledge that responsibility must be based on God's law.

6. James M. Gustafson and James T. Laney, "Introduction," Ibid.

7. Ibid.

8. Ibid. The authors discuss our obligations in terms of commitments, the roles we play in society, as well as the power and authority that we hold.

9. Bonhoeffer, op. cit., 39.

10. Gustafson and Laney discuss this as one of three key questions in responsibility. See also H. Richard Niebuhr, "The Meaning of Responsibility," in *On Being Responsible,* ed. James M. Gustafson and James T. Laney (New York: Harper and Row, 1968).

11. Bernard Haring, "Essential Concepts of Moral Theology," in *On Being Responsible,* ed. James M. Gustafson and James T. Laney (New York: Harper and Row, 1968). Haring uses this term to describe what we owe to others.

12. See Henry Cloud and John Townsend, *Boundaries* (Grand Rapids: Zondervan, 1992).

13. See Gustafson and Laney, "Introduction," in *On Being Responsible,* ed. James M. Gustafson and James T. Laney (New York: Harper and Row, 1968).

Questions for Further Study

1. How do we humans, like Adam, shift the blame for our poor choices to God or to authority figures in our lives? Give examples.
2. Which extreme do you lean toward—forsaking responsibility for your actions or a feeling overly responsible for the actions of others? Give examples from your own life. Why do you think your personality tends toward that extreme?
3. Based on what you learned in this chapter and your previous knowledge, write your own definition of *responsibility*.
4. As quoted in this chapter, Bonhoeffer wrote, ". . . responsibility is the total and realistic response of men to the claim of God and of our neighbor." Give some concrete examples of the claims of God and others.
5. What is the danger of meeting our responsibility to our "neighbors" (other human beings) without regard to God's claims?
6. What happens to an individual who ignores God's claims on his or her life?
7. Why do we, like Adam and Eve, willingly choose to believe the devil's lies rather than God's truth? Why are those lies so attractive to us?
8. Why does responsibility always involve relationships?
9. What is the relationship between freedom and responsibility?
10. How do we determine what our personal responsibilities are?

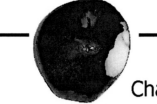

Chapter Two

The Other Side of Responsibility

Words We Hate To Hear

Some time ago I read a newspaper article that was written by a lawyer and entitled "A Thin Excuse for Obesity." The subtitle read: "If everything's a disease, whither responsibility." The author was responding to then Surgeon General C. Everett Koop. Apparently the surgeon general had recently labeled obesity a disease. The author used this occasion as a starting point to attack our society's tendency to ignore responsibility. The author noted: "If everything's a disease, then individually we're responsible for nothing." At another point he noted: "The concept of sin has fallen out of vogue because it carries with it the insinuation that certain acts or omissions are volitional, and that we are therefore at fault if we do them or omit to do them."[1]

Isn't it refreshing to hear a lawyer use words like "sin," "fault," "blame" and "responsibility"? It is to me. Often it seems our court system doesn't take responsibility and blame too seriously, especially if a client has the where-withal to hire a "good" lawyer. We don't take seriously enough responsibility and the fault it implies. The court is just one place where this happens. It's everywhere else. We live in a day of "no-fault alcoholism," "no-fault insurance" and "no-fault divorce." That's just a few examples of things for which our society refuses to ascribe blame.

This avoidance of responsibility may contribute to the widespread use of lawsuits in our society. We seem to be a society that "loves to law." Everyone seems quick to file a lawsuit of some sort. The legal profession contributes to this by advertising that encourages lawsuits for a variety of reasons. But what does this have to do with responsibility? The answer's rather simple: In a society accustomed to avoiding responsibility, lawsuits may be seen as the last resort to hold persons accountable.[2] This reasoning seemed part of the basis behind Paula Jones's sexual harassment suit against President Clinton. Initially Jones claimed she filed suit to get Clinton to accept responsibility. At some points she even offered to withdraw the suit if Clinton would admit to the charges. Apparently she was partly aiming for a show of responsibility on the president's part.

Because we seek to avoid responsibility, we tend to prefer "no-fault" labels. We shy away from words suggesting accountability. At the same time we may have little problem with responsibility's brighter side as seen in words like *relationships, choice, freedom* and *self-awareness.* We may use these words easily and freely. However, we struggle with the other side of responsibility that is reflected in a different set of words. This other side isn't so pleasant to talk about. We may become offended when someone raises the dark side of responsibility, which nobody wants to discuss.

Bad side · Culpability, Guilt,

What are some of these words that we find so troubling? For starters, responsibility always carries the possibility of culpability. *Culpability* comes from the Latin word *culpare*, which means to blame. It means persons can be held responsible for wrong or error. In cases of wrongdoing, we become worthy of censure and blame. But blame isn't an endearing word. For many, it conjures up images of vindictive people trying to get even. Those who take these words seriously are often considered religious bigots, lacking the ability to forgive.

Guilt is another unpleasant word connected to responsibility. When we blame someone, we deem him "guilty" for his actions. Along with the positive aspects of responsibility, blame and guilt both figure prominently in the Genesis account of the Fall. It's fairly obvious that at least in God's eyes, Adam, Eve and the serpent are blameworthy. Because they disobeyed God, they each became guilty. For that, they each received sentence. *A guilty can mean bad, wrong* *This does not mean God abandons them or loves them less*

God's judgment and subsequent sentence introduces us to another negative side of responsibility: guilty persons are judged and punished; irresponsible behavior often does and should lead to negative consequences.

Problems with the Other Side of Responsibility

Some of us have problems with this darker side of responsibility. Except of course, if we were the ones wronged. Then we cry "Foul!" and demand the most severe vengeance. However, much of the time we avoid these words implying blame and guilt. Words like *sin, transgression, judgment* and *punishment* cause us all sorts of trouble. In many sections of our society these words are considered passe, the relics of an archaic religion not relevant to modern folks.

Surprisingly, I find this avoidance tendency even among Christians. It's seen in the tendency to sanitize language and actions. I have seen cases where actions that were clearly wrong and sinful are called "mistakes." Even heinous crimes like murder have been called mistakes. *Mistake* carries little if any responsibility for deeds done. It carries the idea that the offense was more accidental than deliberate. In such cases it's almost as if we are afraid to use the S word. That hesitancy reflects part of our problem with responsibility. Sin is very much related to responsibility. That was part of the emphasis in the lawyer's article. We see this same point in Karl Menninger's *Whatever Became of Sin?* There, he emphasized that "sin traditionally implied guilt, answerability, and, by derivation, responsibility."[3] Sin involves the failure to respond appropriately to the claims of God. It represents the epitome of irresponsible living. Apparently, books like Karl Menninger's are still necessary reading.

Sometimes I wonder if we believe anymore in responsibility and its negative consequences. We seem to absolve people easily for their choices and behaviors. The fellow who becomes a couch potato and amasses great weight has bad genes. The woman who drinks herself into oblivion has a disease. The man who commits murder had a poor childhood. There's some truth in these statements. In cases of obesity and alcoholism some biological predisposition has been documented. But predisposition does not mean predetermination. Even in these cases, there are always choices and behaviors that bring about the undesired consequences.

Much of the time, talk of "no-fault" and "mistakes" serves to absolve individuals of personal responsibility for their choices and behaviors. It gives them the opportunity to say: "You shouldn't blame me. It's not my fault." In so doing, we rob them of the opportunity to become responsibly engaged in creating something new in their lives. They are much poorer because we too quickly free them of the obligation to shape their lives in new ways. In our efforts to free them of blame, guilt, judgment and appropriate consequences, we stunt their growth and potential. Not expecting responsible living is an act of indifference, not love. It is to treat them as less than persons: to condemn them to an unfulfilled life and to doubt their ability to grow in new and healthful ways.

In contrast, when we expect responsibility, we pay the ultimate compliment. We affirm others' personhood and call them to actualize their maximum potential. To call others to responsible living is to express our undying faith in their capacity to reach their potential and to enhance themselves. It's then that we truly relate to them as responsible peers instead of treating them like infants who cannot help themselves.[4] In short, holding persons responsible demonstrates the deepest kind of love. It reflects a commitment to see that they become the best they can be.

Momentarily Siding with God

That's why God holds us responsible. That much is obvious in Genesis. The message in Genesis is responsibility, and this is clear across Scripture. God always holds us squarely responsible. When we make responsible choices and live uprightly, we are living as we should. When we live irresponsibly, we incur blame, guilt and just punishment. Much of the time we seem to stand against God in matters of responsibility. However, sometimes irresponsible actions so outrage us that we momentarily side with God in his view of responsibility.

The shootings and murders at Columbine High School served such a purpose. Suddenly almost everyone, including President Clinton, was speaking about responsibility. In a speech at Virginia Tech following the shootings, Clinton was quoted as saying: "I hate it when people blame others and do not accept responsibility for their behaviors."[5]

Suddenly blame was not such a bad word as we desperately sought answers to this disaster and to assign responsibility. Certainly Harris and Klebold, who did the shooting, deserved blame. Everyone seems to agree with that. But some also pointed fingers at the parents of the youthful killers. How could these parents not have known what their kids were doing? How could they not have known about the bomb-making materials? People asked a lot of questions and much of it concerned responsibility.

The case of Louise Woodward several years ago had similar impact. Some may remember Louise Woodward as the 19-year-old English au pair accused of killing eight-month-old Matthew Eappen. When the jury found her guilty of second-degree murder, it outraged many people in America and Britain. Apparently, many believed her punishment was too severe, even the jury. However, few denied that some punishment was merited. On November 10, 1997, after revisiting the case, Judge Hiller B. Zobel changed the verdict. He ruled Woodward guilty of involuntary manslaughter. Given credit for time served, she was set free after nine months behind bars.

Polls indicated a large number of Americans believed the sentence too lenient. One cartoon jab at the verdict appeared in the local newspaper. In it, a blithe and happy Louise Woodward skips happily along a country road. It's obviously the end of autumn; one last leaf remains to drop from an otherwise barren tree. The color and joy of fall had long since ended. Louise wears a shirt inscribed with her name. Immediately beneath her name, the inscription continued, "Nine months time served." Off to her left, seemingly ignored by Louise, is a more somber scene, one mirroring the dreariness of the season. Next to the road lies a solitary tombstone inscribed with the name Matthew Eappen. Beneath his name the words were written, "Eight months time lived." The contrasts are striking: a blithe, happy, skipping Louise, full of life and vigor presented against the backdrop of a tombstone hiding the promise that was Matthew Eappen, now forever silenced. The cartoonist's message, opinion and anger screams from the page: *The punishment didn't fit the crime*. Apparently, we sometimes still believe in responsibility, in blame and justified punishment.

Perhaps Amy Troubh said it best. Amy was a single mother of two from the affluent suburb of Newton, former home of Matthew Eappen. Troubh was quoted as saying: "I think she should serve some kind of longer term. She killed a baby." Troubh added, "She has not shed a tear over the death of this child. She has not turned to the court and said 'I am sorry for the pain I have caused.'"[6] Troubh comments seemed to reflect the general sentiment on two counts: Louise Woodward did not accept responsibility for the child's death, and she did not receive a just punishment.

Responsibility's Last Word

God still demands responsibility. When we fail, he still calls us to give account. He shows us our fault. He doesn't dilute our guilt in some misguided show of love. He doesn't redirect our blame somewhere else or on someone else. He faces each guilty person squarely. His message is always plain: "You are the man! You are the woman!" He does not allow us to hide from our failed responsibility and our guilt. To hide is to become hopelessly buried in our shame and guilt without remedy.

[handwritten margin notes:] we still feel pain, guilt, but it is held in a greater love from God, who does not abuse us

[handwritten note at bottom:] hiding is bad, we must face it head on

Release from shame involves coming to terms with our responsibility and our guilt.

That's why blame, guilt and just punishment are not the only words spoken about responsibility in the Genesis account. Another word is spoken about the God who preserves us even when we have fallen. In *Creation and Fall*, Bonhoeffer saw God the Creator, acting as the preserver of fallen humanity. He would not leave them in a God-forsaken state with no one or nothing to redeem them. He would act to preserve their lives.[7] He acts to preserve life in every way imaginable, not just physical life. Such preservation also involves releasing humans from toxic shame—the kind of shame that leads us to believe we are thoroughly defective, rotten to the core; unworthy of any redemption. Sometimes this shame makes us run from our choices, behaviors and their consequences by covering up our misdeeds. It leads us to cringe and hide in fear. In so doing, we fail to find much-needed healing and forgiveness. Sometimes, we become so shamed that God has to seek us out to preserve us and forgive us.

I know the word "forgiveness" does not occur in the account. But God, who in grace acts to preserve us, also acts to seek us out and forgive us. Some even infer the possibility of forgiveness in God's act of clothing the couple (Genesis 3:21). The possibility of this forgiveness spells hope for everyone who has failed at responsibility. But it comes with a price; forgiveness always calls us back to live responsibly. Like the woman caught in adultery, we receive freedom from condemnation and punishment. But with it always comes the word, "Go and sin no more."

Made for Responsibility

We really cannot live well without demonstrating responsibility. I suspect we intuitively know its importance to

[margin notes, left side:] God the preserver

[margin notes, left side:] God frees us within sin; God preserves us without; because the want us to grow

[margin notes, left side:] God frees us

[handwritten note beneath boxed text:] we must learn from our experience, respond anew the next time to God forgives and heals

us. That may be the reason we see a renewed call to responsible living in some sections of our society. That's part of the appeal of Promise Keepers. Promise Keepers represents a call to Christian men to live up to their obligations to God and family. Something similar may be said for the marches and gatherings of Black men and women. Their gatherings were largely about taking responsibility for themselves and their future. These groups know responsibility is essential to achieving their potential as God's creatures, as spouses, parents, men and women.

Because we know the critical role responsibility plays, we show disgust when we see irresponsible behavior. That's why so many people were outraged by the Louise Woodward decision described earlier. Because of this, we frown on deadbeat dads like Bufford McIntosh mentioned in Chapter 1. On the other hand, we gain pleasure when we see responsible acts.

I was pleased by a case I read about some time ago. Joseph Hall, 23, had apparently lived irresponsibly at times. He was serving time in Carrollton, Kentucky, for driving without a license. When officers from the Carrollton jail ran his name through a national crime database, they discovered he was wanted for theft in Fayetteville, Georgia.

Given the more serious crime, Hall was to be extradited to Georgia. Two deputies from Georgia picked up Hall. Near the Georgia–Tennessee border, the patrol car hydroplaned, ripped through a guardrail, and soared through the air, crashing through trees in the process. It eventually rolled down a steep hill before coming to a precarious rest. Both deputies sustained serious injuries and were losing consciousness. Strangely enough, Hall emerged from the accident unscathed. However, he broke his foot kicking out the glass in the back of the police cruiser.

Why did he do it? Was this his attempt to escape and
be free again? Hall told the officers: "I'm going to get help.
Please believe me. I promise I'll be back as soon as possible." Though scantily clad in a T-shirt and pants in forty-
degree weather, he climbed the steep, briar-covered in-
cline and, with a broken foot, limped through darkness
and pouring rain for a quarter mile. At last on the high-
way, he flagged a driver who called 911 on his cell phone.
Hall waited for the ambulance and escorted the paramed-
ics back to the injured deputies.[8]

Who would have expected this from Hall? Who would
expect this from someone who had lived irresponsibly?
Yet when it mattered most Hall showed responsibility.
As a result, escape was never an option for him. What
mattered most was getting help for the officers. Such a
deed, characterized by a compassionate response to suffering humanity, must cheer the heart of God. It surely
cheers this human heart. In the aftermath of his heroic
deed, some called Hall a guardian angel. I don't know
about that. Hall had not become an angel but he surely
became more fully human that day.

Because God desires our growth and well being, he
created us for responsibility. Thus, from the dawn of our
creation, God emphasized our need for responsible living. He wove his emphasis on responsibility among other
indisputable human characteristics. For convenience, I
call these the five S's. They include the spiritual, social,
sexual, and survival (life) needs that characterize our days
on earth. Along with those, we may add the need for service (significant work). Genesis features these five areas
prominently in the creation of Adam and Eve. I discuss
these at length in Chapter 5.

God commanded Adam to till and keep the garden.
In a sense, he stood as God's deputy. Along with that
deputyship[9] came a responsibility to God and to the gar-

den. God created Adam and Eve stewards of creation. Stewardship carries with it the idea of responsibility and obligation. They also owed responsibility to God to obey his laws and maintain relationship with him. Early on, God commanded them not to eat of the fruit of the tree of life. To do so would be to forfeit relationship. Adam and Eve also carried responsibility for themselves and to each other.

Thus, like the five S's, responsibility forms an intrinsic part of the fabric of our lives. That's why we find it nestled among these other essential elements of human life. Actually *nestled* may not be the best word. Responsibility is firmly *entwined* with each of these S's. These are essential areas in which we must be responsible. When we succeed, our lives become richer. When we fail, we become much poorer.

We see the latter truth lived out in Adam and Eve. Failing at responsibility, their lives became diminished: They shamed themselves; they lost fellowship with God; their lives were shortened; they experienced drastic changes in their quality of life and surroundings. Life became a chore and a grind, all because they failed to live responsibly! We cannot begin to imagine how much richer their lives might have been had they done the responsible thing.

A Lesson from Pinocchio

I suspect Carlo Collodi knew something of these truths when he wrote *The Adventures of Pinocchio*. Each act of irresponsibility made the wooden puppet less humanlike. For instance, each lie made his nose grow longer to the point of being grotesque. Only speaking the truth, a responsible behavior, could return his nose to its natural state. Likewise, disobedience to his father made him sprout ears like a donkey. Collodi knew that irresponsible actions make us less than we are. We become more like marionettes dangling on the Devil's string. Collodi also knew living responsibly enriches us. Thus, it took a supremely responsible act finally to transform Pinocchio into a real flesh and blood boy. If you remember the story, you know Pinocchio became human after he saved his father's life.

Perhaps there's a parallel truth for us. Without responsible living, we either become shadows of our real selves or distortions of what God intended. With responsible choices and behaviors, we become more than we are; more fully human, more of what God intended us to be. That's why God made us for responsibility.

Endnotes

1. Frank M. Jenkins III, "A Thin Excuse for Obesity," *Lexington Herald-Leader,* November 29, 1996.

2. I am indebted to my former doctoral chair, Dr. John F. Wilson, for this thought. I gained this insight during a conversation with him on this topic.

3. Karl Menninger, *Whatever Became of Sin?* (New York: Hawthorne Books, 1974), 20.

4. Ferdinand Schoeman, *Responsibility, Character and Emotions* (New York: Cambridge University Press), 1987.

5. Bill Clinton in a speech made at Virginia Tech in the wake of the shooting at Columbine High School in Littleton, Colorado.

6. Both the cartoon and the article "Many Call Judge in Au Pair Case too Lenient" appeared in the *Lexington-Herald Leader,* November 12, 1997.

7. Dietrich Bonhoeffer, *Creation and Fall: A Theological Exposition of Genesis 1–3,* D. S. Bax, trans. (Minneapolis: Fortress Press, 1997).

8. Associated Press, "Prisoner Helps Rescue GA Officers after Crash," *Lexington-Herald Leader,* November 9, 1997, B8.

9. See Bonhoeffer, "The Structure of Responsible Life," in *On Being Responsible,* ed. James M. Gustafson and James T. Laney (New York: Harper and Row, 1968). Bonhoeffer discusses responsibility

in terms of deputyship. By it, he meant that one ". . . is directly obligated to act in the place of other men," p. 39. He saw Jesus as assuming deputyship for all persons and subsequently passing on that requirement to all.

Questions for Further Study

1. Do you agree with the author that the widespread use of lawsuits in our society may reveal our avoidance of responsibility? Why or why not?
2. List as many of the positive words associated with responsibility as you can, beginning with the author's suggestions. Next, list all the negative words related to responsibility that you can think of, again using the author's suggestions to get you started.
3. Why do we seek mercy for our own irresponsible acts and yet demand vengeance for trespasses against us?
4. Explain the difference between committing a sin and making a mistake.
5. According to the author, what do we "rob" people of when we absolve them of all personal responsibility for their choices and behavior?
6. What does the author mean when he refers to "toxic shame"?
7. The author points to *The Adventures of Pinocchio* as an example of a popular literary work that illustrates the relationship between accepting responsibility and becoming more fully human. Can you think of other examples from literature or films that illustrate this relationship? Explain your choices.

Chapter Three

Responsible to Whom?

I n the spring of 1997, my eldest son Jon attended Ichthus, the annual Christian music festival. When he returned, he was wearing a green cloth bracelet bearing the letters "WWJD." Not knowing what that meant, I inquired. He told me the letters stood for "What Would Jesus Do?" The youth leaders had given the bracelet to members of the group. They wanted teenagers to ask this question when confronted with tempting situations.

Since that time, I have seen the bracelet and other jewelry bearing those letters almost everywhere. They became part of popular fashion for Christian youth. I have even seen adults wearing them. George was one such adult. He had been a leader within the Christian community in a small Kentucky town. I was aware of some key events in his life. He had not lived responsibly in recent months. He had become involved in a short sexual fling with another woman. In the process, he had failed God, his wife and son, plus many people who respected him.

George had sought forgiveness and was trying to grapple anew with responsibility. I asked George about the bracelet. He said: "I wear it to remind myself that Jesus is my standard for behavior."

The bracelets speak about Christian responsibility. Though somewhat trendy, the question "What would Jesus do?" is a significant one. It highlights our need of a guide for determining responsible behavior. More importantly, it points to Jesus as that ultimate guideline. WWJD also suggests a fundamental question about responsibility. In the first chapter, I noted that we should ask, "What is my responsibility?" Now let's add another question: "To whom am I responsible?"[1]

"What would Jesus do?" partly speaks to this question. These words remind us we are not a law unto ourselves. They point to the primary One to whom we must give account. We serve a higher law; we must turn to Jesus Christ if we would learn to live responsibly. It's from him that we derive rules for appropriate conduct. Only by looking to God in Jesus Christ do we have a real basis for responsible living.

In addition to God in Christ, we owe other obligations. Briefly stated, we owe three responsibilities to persons (four if we include our obligations to the rest of creation).[2]

1. We owe responsibility to God (and to his created order).
2. We owe responsibility to ourselves.
3. We are co-responsible to our neighbors.

Our first responsibility to God is to know, love, obey and enjoy God. As part of our original mandate from God, we are to protect creation lovingly. Second, to other humans, we owe the obligation of loving service. Third, Randy Maddox notes that when these relationships are properly exercised, we have a proper relationship to our-selves, that of self-acceptance.[3]

These obligations form a triad for responsible living, as pictured in the following diagram:

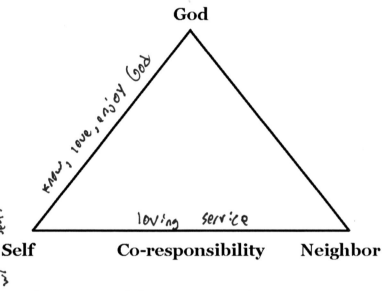

God

know, love, enjoy God

loving service

Self   **Co-responsibility**   **Neighbor**

proper relationship w/ self.

These responsibilities appear in the creation account in Genesis. Clearly, Adam and Eve owed primary respon-sibility to God. In fact, God's first recorded word to hu-mans involved a call to responsibility. God had laid his claims on their lives. In Genesis 1:28, they were called to several tasks:

1. To have dominion over the earth and creation   - *responsibility*
2. To be fruitful and multiply — *responsibility*
3. To subdue the earth — *responsibility*
4. To fill the earth   — *responsibility.*

These tasks placed explicit responsibilities on Adam and Eve. They owed obligations to God and to his cre-ated order. We find additional responsibilities laid on Adam in 2:15–17. Genesis 2:15 gives a new twist to Adam's rule over the earth. In the garden, a microcosm of the earth, we learn that the relationship involves work of and care for the earth. The commands also imply their mutual obligations to each other. Even in these early commands, we note this triad of responsibilities: To God (and creation), to self and to each other.

We see an additional obligation placed on Adam in Genesis 2:16–17. There we read: "And the LORD God commanded the man, saying, 'You may freely eat of every tree of the garden; but of the tree of the knowledge of good and evil you shall not eat, for in the day that you eat of it you shall die.'" This verse highlights the responsibility to obey God.

The command and subsequent events prove that they also owed obligations to themselves and to each other. Adam and Eve were individually responsible for their conduct. This is so apparent that few would debate it. Each needed to demonstrate obedience to God for his or her own good. However, since their lives were integrally bound together, each needed to obey for the other's good. They owed the other co-responsibility.[4] Co-responsibility means that Adam *shared* some responsibility for Eve. Eve also shared some responsibility for Adam. Co-responsibility points to the sharedness of human life. It suggests that one's choices and behaviors can deeply affect others. Thus, Eve's failure to obey would have consequences for Adam as well as for herself. Likewise, Adam's sin would affect Eve and all their offspring as well as himself.

This highlights an awesome reality: We never disobey God and affect only ourselves. Individual disobedience, whatever form it takes, always affects others. People's lives are constantly linked. Our lives are bound together. Because of this bondedness, we owe each other co-responsibility. This is especially true in marriage and family relationships.

A Necessary Tension

Responsibility to God, self and others must always be considered together. When we overemphasize one and exclude the others, irresponsible living is not far off. In fact, faulty beliefs and behaviors occur when any part of the triad is neglected. The danger appears more evident when we emphasize responsibility to self or others. However, similar problems occur when we emphasize responsibility to God and forget self and others. *love God, love people, can't have one without the other*

Some popular slogans reflect our problems with holding the three responsibilities together. For instance, we often hear slogans such as: "If it feels good, do it"; "Nobody is going to tell me what to do"; and "Always look out for number one!" We all know who number one is. These slogans reflect an emphasis on responsibility to oneself without due regard to God or others. When we live this way, we become a law unto ourselves. We bow only at our own shrines. We refuse to acknowledge obligations to any other. One of my colleagues calls this "setting up the kingdom of the self."[5] In this stance, only responsibility to oneself matters. Nothing and no one else matters. Typically, becoming a law to oneself leads to exploitation of and tyranny over others. These actions violate others to benefit the self.[6] Even when such persons act on behalf of others, their underlying goal is ultimately to benefit the self. *the American Dream* *believe we overemphasize self, we only look to our own selves*

This self-serving attitude appears evident in Jesus' parable of the unjust judge (Luke 18:1–8). The parable primarily teaches about prayer. However, it also reveals the judge's selfishness and total disregard for God and others. He finally rendered justice to the widow solely for his own purposes. That's evident in verses 4–5:

> For a while he refused; but afterward he said to himself, "Though *I neither fear God nor regard man*, yet

because this widow bothers me, I will vindicate her, or *she will wear me out by her continual coming"* (italics mine).

The judge's decision had little to do with justice. Rather his decision served himself. He thought nothing of God or the widow's dire needs—only his convenience and comfort. Some people act like the judge. They show no responsibility to God or others. They serve only the self.

Iago, the bird in Disney's *Aladdin,* serves as a popular example of one who looks out primarily for number one. He constantly looks out for his own interests, even forsaking his friends. In the movie, *The Return of Jafar,* Iago finally puts his deep selfishness into words when he complains: "I am not responsible to anyone but myself." So say all who worship only at their own shrine. Iago, the bird, is very much like his earlier namesake, Iago from Shakespeare's *Othello.* Like the bird, Iago looks out only for number one. But he is much more sinister than the bird. For his own gain, he lies and plots the destruction of Desdemona and Othello. At the end, he is done in by his own evil.

Overemphasizing responsibility to others leads to similar problems. When another person becomes the absolute, all other obligations, including responsibilities owed to God and self, are ignored or neglected.[7] One form of this over-responsibility can be termed myopic or nearsighted; it so focuses on responsibility to one person that it ignores obligations to others. This often leads to disastrous consequences.

Not too long ago I watched a television biography of Nicholas and Alexandra, the last Romanov rulers of Russia. They were the parents of Anastasia, the title character in Disney's movie of the same name. However, the movie bears little resemblance to real life.

Judging by the biography, Nicholas and Alexandra suffered from a myopic sense of responsibility: Their son, Alexie, happened to be a hemophiliac, a "bleeder" in common terminology. Nicholas and Alexandra showed extreme concern for their son's health. Sometimes grave national issues got lost in the shuffle. The program suggested their connection to the evil Rasputin flowed from concern for their son's health. They believed Rasputin to be a healer who could help their son. Therefore, he became a confidant and advisor. Following his advice led to disastrous consequences for the nation. It evidently played a role in their ultimate murder.

Another form of over-responsibility involves following one person exclusively. Sometimes this can lead to sinister results, as it did for the Nazi movement. Following Hitler, many top generals gave orders for the extermination of millions of Jews. Ironically, some insisted that they had acted responsibly. Adolf Eichman made this claim when he was tried for his crimes before an Israeli court. In his defense, he said that he was acting under orders and thereby being responsible to his Nazi superiors. *A that is a worldly law,*

Sometimes it's not so much responsibility to a person *not c* but to a cause. The consequences are just as grim. The *Godly one* events of 911 speak to this. Nineteen men, dedicated to Islamic *jihad* as spouted by Osama Bin Laden, were willing to destroy themselves in an effort to kill Americans. Close to three thousand people died because of this misguided commitment to a cause. The Oklahoma bombing is another tragic example. Timothy McVeigh evidently felt committed to a cause and rebelled against what he saw as unwanted government intrusion. This misshapen sense of responsibility devalued human life. As a result 168 persons, including innocent children, died.

But what if we focus on responsibility to God without attention to self and others? At first this might appear a good thing. It is not. One cannot really respond to God and forget human life. Responsibility to the invisible God almost always means responding lovingly to visible people. Living out our obligations to God means serving our own and others' well-being. To do anything else is to misunderstand God.

Unfortunately, many of us often misunderstand God and our responsibilities to him. Some of us believe we can ignore, neglect or hurt others and be responsible to God. One example might suffice. Not too long ago, I sat in the waiting room of a car company while my vehicle was being repaired. While I waited, a talk show aired. The program's focus on the KKK caught my attention. The first guest was a grand dragon. He claimed to be a preacher. He proceeded to spout Scripture justifying hatred of and crimes against people different from himself. Several others, men and women, also appealed to their religious convictions. They obviously felt that they were showing responsibility to God. Actually, I got the impression that they felt that they defended God. They claimed to serve God with little regard for the life and dignity of others.

Failing to hold the three responsibilities together usually leads to irresponsible choices and behaviors. (The chart on the next page summarizes these problems.) Perhaps that's why God chose to emphasize his claims on our lives *together with* claims on us from self and neighbor. That much appears evident in the Ten Commandments (Exodus 20:2–17). God's claims and those of self and neighbor appear together. We find the same coupling in the Great Commandment. Jesus decreed:

> "You shall love the Lord your *God* with all your heart, and with all your soul, and with all your mind. This is the great and first commandment. And a second is like

A Three-fold Failure at Responsibility

GOD

Responsibility exclusively to God—evil is carried out in the name of God (represents misunderstanding of God)

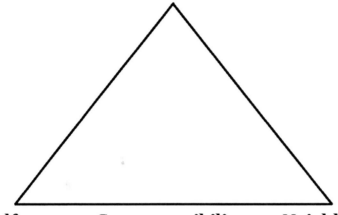

Self   **Co-responsibility**   **Neighbor**

*Absolute autonomy
—responsibility only
to self; being law unto
self—"the kingdom
of the self"*

*Absolute obligations
to others; responsible
exclusively to other
person(s) or cause,
for example, the Nazi
movement*

it, You shall love your *neighbor* as *yourself*. On these two commandments depend all the law and the prophets" (Matthew 22:37–40, italics mine).

Being responsible to God means living responsively to self and neighbor. Anything else constitutes irresponsible living. *you cannot do one and not the other*

We Are Responsible to God

Note that I placed responsibility to God at the top of the triangle. This doesn't contradict balancing responsibilities to God, self and neighbor; rather, it indicates the order and priority for responsible living. We cannot live appropriately without first acknowledging our obligations to God. That's why the Ten Commandments and the Great Commandment both begin with our obligations to God. In the Ten Commandments, the first four cover God's claims on our lives. In the Great Commandment, our first obligation is to love God with all our hearts. God is the one who sets the norms and limits of human responsibility.

But why do we first owe responsibility to God? A thoughtful person could suggest several good reasons. For brevity, I have chosen just three to discuss.

1. Living Responsibly Before God Acknowledges Our Lives as Creatures

God created us. We did not create ourselves. As Paul proclaimed to the Athenians, "In him [God] we live and move and have our being, as even some of your poets have said, 'For we are indeed his offspring'" (Acts 17:28). As God's creatures we depend on him for our very lives. There is no life apart from him. We owe him our life. It's when we fail to acknowledge our creaturely nature that we live irresponsibly as a law unto ourselves, as though we created ourselves. We live as though God does not matter and that we alone matter. That's a recipe for disaster. One look at Adam and Eve and their fall tells us that.

On the other hand, if we acknowledge God as our creator, then we readily see that we owe our first responsibility to him, just as a young child owes responsibility to the parents who gave him life. Thus, one author wrote:

> Because a man's dependence on God is so much greater than a child's dependence on his parents, so there is a duty to a man to make much more of his life pleasing to God than there is a duty on the child to make his life pleasing to his parents.[8]

That's what we see in the creation account. God laid claims on Adam and Eve because they were his creatures. Yet he also gave them the freedom to respond to these claims. And even though they acted otherwise, God's claims were intended for their good. Responding to these claims was the means to the enrichment of their lives.

2. Our Responsibility to God Serves Our Deepest Needs and Interests

because we are creatures created by God, we choose to respond with our ability first to Him

Responsibility to God also answers our deepest needs. Because we are his creatures, he knows our needs. He issues his commands to serve those needs. Thus, God's prohibition against eating from the tree of good and evil is not about restraining us. Rather, it primarily involves saving us, spiritually and physically. True, it involves the language of prohibition. But it's prohibition with a promise of life.

heals our deepest wounds, restores us

God knows our needs past surface level, needs that will give us abundant life

One could also argue that responding to him makes us like him. Such responsible behavior makes his image in us an increasing reality. We become shaped into the image of holiness. No wonder God commanded: "Be holy, for I am holy" (Leviticus 11:44; 1 Peter 1:16). His commands call us to become our best, being and acting like him.

Responsibility to God also meets our interests. The command in Genesis 1:28 serves as a good example. Responding to his claims was intended for our good and was not primarily intended for God's benefit. Thus, each of the four commands in that verse speaks of human enhancement and growth. This should not surprise us. Since he created us, God shows interest in our growth and enhancement. He also actively works for our greatest good. Like a good father, God always provides us with opportunity to make something of ourselves. He encourages us to fulfill our potential. When we fail to live up to our potential, we disappoint him.[9]

He created us and said we are good

3. God Provides the Ultimate Standards for Responsible Living

There's another reason to respond first to God: God provides the ultimate standards. He laid out the directives for the responsible life. Failing to respond to God as our first priority leaves us lost and without appropriate limits and guidance. Without him, we lose contact with reality.

No wonder God provided us with both a written word and a living word. The written word refers to scriptural teachings that tell us what life is all about. Following those teachings helps us to live responsibly. But God also provided us with a living Word, Jesus Christ. He stands as the eternal example of responsible living. Bonhoeffer appropriately called Jesus: "The responsible person *par excellence*."[10] He provided the ultimate example of showing responsibility to God, self and neighbor. By looking at him we learn how to live a responsible life.

That's why the question "What would Jesus do?" is so significant. Through its consideration, we find the eternal standard for behavior in the One whose actions involve supreme responsibility. When we take this question seriously, responsible living is not very far away. By following Jesus, we discover that we, too, can live responsibly. Jesus is indeed the responsible man par excellence. Anyone following him and his teachings closely becomes a responsible person. Responsibility is indeed fulfilled when Christ is our center and we live committed to him.[11]

We Are Responsible to Ourselves

We owe responsibility to God but also to ourselves. That's easier said than done. The journey to appropriate self-responsibility demands charting a path between a morbid self-focus and an over-focus on others, leading to self neglect. Sometimes we drift towards *an over-focus on the self.* That is, we can become a law unto ourselves, ignoring all other obligations. In many cases this self-focus is reactive. It springs from a desperate attempt to compensate for focusing too much on others. At other times, it flows from earlier failures to show appropriate responsibility for oneself. Generally these failures fall into two categories: neglecting responsibility to the self and delegating too much responsibility for the self to others.

We can also act irresponsibly by *an over-focus on others.* Kathy, mentioned in the first chapter, serves as a good example. She spent much of her time and energy covering Kim's misdeeds. As a result, she freed Kim to continue to live irresponsibly. At the same time, Kathy had little time to fulfill obligations to herself. Thus, we find in Kathy two problems in responsibility: over-functioning for Kim and under-functioning for herself. This should not surprise us. Over-responsibility for others and under-responsibility for oneself often go hand in hand; by focusing on others, we are able to ignore much of our obligation to ourselves. Both problems generally represent irresponsible living.

Unfortunately, some Christians tend to see these problems as spiritual virtues. Some identify over-responsibility for others with essential Christian living. They often quote Galatians 6:2, "Bear one another's burdens, and so fulfil the law of Christ," as justification. They fail to notice the later verse that says each person shall bear his own burdens (Galatians 6:5). This balance suggests co-responsibility, not exclusive responsibility to oneself or neighbor. To compound the problem, some Christians also associate responsibility to oneself as selfish. They almost believe that showing responsibility to oneself constitutes sin. Nothing could be further from the truth.

Why should we emphasize responsibility to oneself? Let's explore three reasons for self-responsibility.

1. Self-Responsibility Is
Essential to Spiritual Health

Individual responsibility determines spiritual health and destiny. That's always been the case. Thus, Ezekiel wrote:

> The soul that sins shall die. The son shall not suffer for the iniquity of the father, nor the father suffer for the iniquity of the son; the righteousness of the righteous shall be upon himself, and the wickedness of the wicked shall be upon himself (Ezekiel 18:20).

Ezekiel's words speak about personal responsibility and consequences. They demonstrate that persons bear primary responsibility for their own salvation and spiritual health. We cannot take this responsibility lightly without experiencing the most extreme consequences. On it hangs the difference between heaven and hell. Thus, in relation to salvation, we always owe greater responsibility to ourselves than to others.[12] Only we can decide how we respond to God's offer of salvation. *A ?? Not sure*

This responsibility applies to other areas, not only to spiritual well-being. In fact, responsibility determines overall health and well-being. Without it, we never experience growth in any area of our lives. I have seen this continually in the counseling room: Those persons who assume responsibility for their lives experience emotional healing. Those who refuse responsibility stay bound in emotional pain.

The same applies to physical health. No one ever experiences physical healing without it. My friend, Mark, a medical doctor, tells how some of his patients who suffer from emphysema and other lung diseases insist on medications to treat their problems, yet they refuse to give up smoking. Their choices and behaviors obviously play a big role in their condition.

2. Self-Responsibility Is the Only Way to Maintain Moral Integrity Before God

God created us with the capacity to distinguish between right and wrong. That's part of our moral nature. Being moral creatures requires that we choose between good and evil. It requires choice and decision. We cannot remain morally neutral. Perhaps that's why God commanded Adam and Eve to choose between good and evil. He required a responsible choice. Moral creatures must always make moral choices. They must either choose the good or the evil. Each choice confirms character. By choosing the good, we lay out a path for further growth in goodness. Our decision to choose evil or to refuse to choose good defiles our nature and corrupts our character.

God also created us creatures of integrity. Integrity carries two main thoughts. One relates to our moral nature. In this sense, it carries the idea of soundness or moral uprightness. Applied to Adam and Eve, it means that God created them without sin or moral corruptness. By making right choices and doing the right thing, they would maintain and enhance this standing before God. God expected this from them. He expected them to make godly choices consistently. He desired that they conform their conduct and character to godly mandates and thus become people of integrity. They owed it to themselves and to God to maintain this moral integrity, and they could only maintain it by living responsibly.

The second thought in integrity points to completeness or wholeness. We often use the word in this sense when we speak of a building's structural integrity. By that, we mean that the building is complete; it is fit to inhabit without fear of its collapsing. This sense of integrity also applied to Adam and Eve. Before their fall, they evidently possessed a wholeness and completeness we do not possess.

(margin note: But we are in large while relationship have been broke)

What happens when we fail to live responsibly? We experience a loss of moral integrity and become morally corrupt. That's loss of integrity in the first sense of the word. But we also experience a loss of integrity in the second sense. Our lives begin to fall apart. Instead of wholeness, we experience fragmentation. We become *disintegrated*, broken creatures. Much of the time, this fragmentation flows through our whole being, affecting body, mind, spirit and relationships. I shall speak more about this in a later chapter.

3. Responsibility to Self Is Important for Becoming a Whole Person

Integrity in the sense of completeness highlights responsibility's role in becoming a whole person. E. L. Mascall highlighted this in his book, *The Importance of Being Human*. Mascall associates personhood with our spiritual nature. We possess the capacity for personhood because God, in whose image we are created, is supremely personal. Furthermore, for Mascall, being a person involves having the capacity to make free and responsible decisions and the ability to give oneself to others in those decisions.[13] When we make responsible decisions and give of ourselves, we realize our full selves.

That's exactly the message of Pinocchio. Pinocchio became a real boy only after he saved his father's life. In that act, he gave himself, risking his own life. Without such behavior, he could never become human. It took that behavior to bring the promise of becoming a real boy to bloom. A similar transformation takes place in us. We become more than we presently are; we become more what we were intended to become. That's because living responsibly is all about achieving our potential as persons, becoming creatively involved in contributing to what we become.[14] But the opposite is also true;

we detract from our potential and our nature when we live irresponsibly. Becoming a whole person means becoming like God. We were created in his image—created to be like him. Becoming what some call a "fully functioning person" comes through responding positively to God's plan for our lives. In short, it means responsible surrender to all his revealed will.

We Are Co-responsible for Our Neighbors

You may remember the callousness of David Cash Jr., a nineteen-year-old University of California, Berkeley, student. In May 1997 Cash watched while his friend Jeremy Strohmeyer attacked seven-year-old Sherrice Iverson in a Las Vegas restroom. He walked away without attempting to stop the attack or report it. Strohmeyer proceeded to sexually molest and strangle Sherrice. Cash showed no remorse for his Sherrice's death or his inaction on her behalf. In an interview with the *Los Angeles Times*, Cash defiantly stated: "I'm not going to get upset over someone else's life. I just worry about myself first." Cash went on to express sympathy for his friend Strohmeyer. In reference to Sherrice's death, he said that he was not going to lose sleep over someone else's problems.[15]

Incidents like this emphasize the need to be responsible for others. We cannot ignore the plight of others while lost in our own selfish worlds. We must become co-responsible for our neighbors.[16]

I need to clarify two things about this co-responsibility for our neighbors. First, as noted earlier, co-responsibility points to *shared* responsibility. That's always true whenever we encounter our neighbor. Responsibility for neighbors is shared because we have no direct control over them as we do ourselves. We cannot control our neighbors' choices, values or actions. That's even true when a neighbor is someone close to us such as a spouse or child. A parent may have a greater degree of control over a young child. (Although one wonders about that when observing parents in public places whose children are throwing temper tantrums.) As the child grows into adulthood, parents have less control. In reality, we always have limited control in others' lives. Because of this limitation, we are called to live co-responsibly, not to assume full responsibility for our neighbors. Co-responsibility with adults could mean any of the following: imparting wisdom, offering advice, warning and praying for our neighbor. Co-responsibility does not mean that my neighbor and I bear *equal* responsibility for his choices and actions. My neighbor must assume the greater weight for these. The exception is when responsibility involves *my attitudes and actions toward my neighbor*. I bear primary responsibility because they are my attitudes and my actions.

[margin handwritten note: And not equal responsibility for choices and actions]

Neighbor: Anyone in Need

The second term requiring clarification is *neighbor*. Here I use the term in the sense found in the parable of the Good Samaritan (Luke 10:25–37). This parable forms a story about responsible and irresponsible behavior and answers two fundamental questions.

The first obvious question forms the basis for the parable. "Who is my neighbor?" asked the lawyer, seeking to justify himself. Jesus' gave a plain answer: Your neighbor is anyone in need, whether that person is near or far. From the description in the story, it seems fairly obvious that the wounded man was a Jew. This made the response of the Samaritan even more astounding. After all, Jews like this wounded man hated Samaritans. This Jew might even have refused the Samaritan's aid had he not been badly wounded.

This cultural barrier based on the Jew's hatred tells us something about co-responsibility: Such actions transcend cultural, racial and religious barriers. We can never say to God without incurring guilt, "I could not respond to my neighbor because she was not of my group." That will not do. Co-responsibility always means that I must respond to people in need when I have the capacity to meet those needs. Apparently David Cash, Jr., did not believe this as he cruelly ignored young Sherrice's plight.

Exerting co-responsibility involves both my response to my neighbor and his response to me. In the parable, the Samaritan responded to the wounded Jew. However, the Samaritan could have done nothing if the Jew refused the offer of aid. Both the Samaritan and the Jew's response were necessary for the obligation of aid to be fulfilled. We must remember this truth: We can never really exert direct co-responsibility to our neighbor unless she is willing. When neighbors refuse our offers of aid, we can take few direct actions. Any co-responsibility must then use indirect means such as prayer on their behalf.

A true story may illustrate what I mean. In 1980 while a seminary student, I pastored a church in Paris, Kentucky. Like many pastors, I often received calls from people in need. One such call came from a man stranded at a local Hardee's restaurant. His car had broken down. He had no money or the means to get home. Not quite knowing what to expect, I got a couple of older teens from my church to accompany me to Hardee's to meet the man. He was a small, slender white man, disheveled in appearance and obviously in need. After some conversation about his situation, I offered to take him to Lexington, about twenty miles away. I also offered to get him a bus ticket that would get him home. He appeared quite interested in my offer. However, as we continued to speak, his wife drew near. She was a rather large woman. Behind her came an equally large son. When she saw that I am black, she refused to go along with the plan. The man, being desperate, said he would go anyway. She immediately threatened him: "If you do, I will call the police and tell them you abandoned us." Her threat and size prevailed. I could not help them even though I was willing.

The parable also answers a second question about responsibility: "What do I owe my neighbor?" I suggest that we owe two things: First, we owe our neighbors compassionate love. Second, we need to meet our neighbors' needs, not their wants.

We Owe Compassionate Love to Our Neighbor

There's a reason for mentioning compassion. In the parable, compassion represents the difference between the Samaritan, the priest and the Levite. The Samaritan showed it; the priest and Levite did not. Compassion plays a large role in whether we show co-responsibility to our neighbor. Always when we show appropriate compassion, we act co-responsibly for our neighbor. Thus, some responsible action to one's neighbor is assumed in each instance where compassion is highlighted in the Synoptic gospels. For example, in Luke's gospel, the word *compassion* occurs three times. The first reference appears in 7:13 in the story of the widow of Nain. Jesus' compassion for her led him to raise her son to life. The second reference occurs in 15:20. There the word refers to the compassion of the prodigal's father that led him to receive his wayward son joyously. The third reference appears in this parable of the Good Samaritan (Luke 10:33). The word is used only of the Samaritan. That attitude led him to care for the wounded Jew. One must also surmise that the lack of compassion led the priest and the Levite to ignore their Jewish brother in need.

Significantly, ten of the fourteen direct references to compassion in the Synoptic Gospels apply to Jesus. Jesus acted compassionately toward others. His compassion always led to meeting others' needs. Thus, we read in Mark 6:34: "As he went ashore he saw a great throng, and he had compassion on them, because they were like sheep without a shepherd; and he began to teach them many things." This type of service to others characterizes Jesus' compassionate action in the other gospels. For example, in Matthew 9:36, he prayed for the multitude who seemed as sheep without a shepherd; in Matthew 14:14, he healed the sick; in Matthew 15:32, he fed four thousand people; and in Matthew 20:24, he healed two blind men.

[margin handwriting: compassion leads to meeting needs and not surface needs, but deep needs for wholeness and redemption, restoration and healing]

In part, it's this compassionate life that makes Jesus the "responsible man *par excellence.*" Behind his responsible actions beats a compassionate heart. This allows him to see each person as created in God's image, even when that image is tremendously marred by sin. For Jesus, compassion was love on wheels; love that impelled him to meet the variety of human needs that crossed his path. God calls us to the same.

[margin handwriting: compassion was the vehicle that allowed Jesus to see people as people, and to fulfill needs]

To Meet Human Needs Is Not to Take Over Others' Lives

The parable of the Good Samaritan concerns needs, not wants. The wounded Jew had legitimate needs. That's why the priest's and Levite's failure to respond constituted irresponsibility. The priest seemed totally callous to suffering humanity. The Levite was characterized by idle curiosity—he was curious enough to view the bloody scene, but not to render responsible aid. Both religious persons lacked sufficient compassion to see a creature of God, a fellow human, in the mass of blood and wounds. Failing to see his humanity made it difficult for them to see his need.

[margin handwriting: when we dehumanize, we no longer see a person like us, in need of reconciliation]

On the other hand, the Samaritan saw both the humanity and the need. In the wounded Jew, he did not see an enemy—a cultural, racial bigot. He saw a fellow human. Thus, he could respond to the man as a human, not as an enemy, and easily saw his need. These two elements—seeing another's humanity and seeing his needs—makes for co-responsibility. Without these we tend to act in a bestial manner toward others, failing to live compassionately and co-responsibly with our neighbors.

Mike Tyson's debacle a few years ago partly illustrates this. In his fight with Evander Holyfield, Mike Tyson furiously mauled both ears of his opponent. He bit off part of one ear and spat it out on the boxing floor. Then he went after the other ear. I was intrigued by a recent interview with Mike Tyson in which he sought to explain his behavior. He conceded: "I shouldn't have done that. It was just striking out and total hatred right there. I shouldn't have done that because for that one moment, *I just forgot he was a human being*" (italics mine).

Boxing's brutality aside, once Holyfield's humanity was obscured, Tyson's bestial act became possible. Gone was any sense of his opponent's need for dignity and reasonable treatment. This same ignoring of humanity contributed to the enslavement of Africans in our country. Once black slaves were considered less than human, slave masters felt justified in any action they took against them.

Thus, we must always attempt to see others' humanity and to respond co-responsibly. This also means seeing another person as a fellow creature of God, one who deserves to have his or her needs met. Any other perception allows murder, torture and enslavement of others. In the parable the focus was on physical needs. We could call these survival needs. However, people also possess spiritual, social and psychological needs. These needs sometimes go deeper than one's physical needs.

In *Responsibility and Atonement,* Richard Swinburne discussed responsibility to neighbor as involving positive and negative duties.[17] Positive duties refer to those things that we ought to do for our neighbor; they represent acts of commission. Negative duties refer to actions we ought to avoid; they represent acts of omission. These constitute the minimal duties that we owe to each other. In addition, we also owe obligations to our benefactors. I list these below:

1. Positive duties—"Love that works no ill"
   a. Tell the truth
   b. Keep promises (including all obligations, including love, debts, etc.)

2. Negative duties—violations of human personal integrity
   a. Murder
   b. Torture
   c. Rape
   d. Theft

3. Obligations to benefactors
   a. Duties of children to obey parents—we owe a debt of gratitude to those who have conserved or given to us the gift of life[18]

One may readily note that these duties relate well to the Ten Commandments. They represent the expression of love that does not work ill to one's neighbor.

How Do You Spell Joy?

You will notice the order in which I discussed responsibility God, self and others. That's deliberate. It might not sit well with some Christian readers. Most believe the order should be God, others and self. To quote a popular acronym: Jesus, others and you spells J-O-Y.

I do not disagree that God must be first. That's the only way to be in touch with reality and to know what the real standards are. In fact, that's the only way to become a fully functioning person created in the image of God. Furthermore, any possibility for becoming a loving person begins with God. It begins with experiencing his love for us and responding to that love.

However, our next critical responsibility is to love ourselves. In a recent Sunday school class, our teacher quoted Bernard of Clairvaux on this topic. For Bernard of Clairvaux, the highest form of human love involved loving ourselves for God's sake. That is, loving ourselves because God first loved us. That makes good spiritual and psychological sense. There is a deep sense in which we can never love another until we know how to love ourselves. People who do not love themselves find it difficult to respond to others. They do not know how to give and receive love.

I have seen countless examples of this in therapy. Jesus had this love of self in mind when he gave the second Great Commandment. Too many persons treat this verse as though self-love were an afterthought. Many don't even acknowledge a scriptural place for loving oneself. They forget the "as yourself." To me, Jesus indicated that we love others by applying the same gracious patterns to others that we do to ourselves. Knowing how to perform loving actions to the self becomes the pattern that we apply to our neighbor. That place for loving self is always assumed in Scripture. No wonder Paul wrote: "Even so husbands should love their wives as their own bodies. He who loves his wife loves himself. For no man ever hates his own flesh, but nourishes and cherishes it, as Christ does the church" (Ephesians 5:28–29)." For Paul, loving self is a given. How we love ourselves ought to become the pattern for

*Maybe, maybe, it can be others before self, though

how we love our wives—or anyone else. When we understand this, we enter a path that permits responsible living to God, self and others.

Endnotes

1. See H. Richard Niebuhr, "On Being Responsible," in *On Being Responsible*, ed. James M. Gustafson and James T. Laney (New York: Harper and Row, 1968).

2. Randy L. Maddox, *Responsible Grace* (Nashville: Abingdon, 1994). Maddox refers to John Wesley's relational anthropology as involving four basic relationships: with God, other humans, lower animals and oneself (p. 68 ff.). I have spoken about three by subsuming our obligation to creation along with our obligations to God.

3. Ibid., p. 68.

4. Bernard Haring, "Essential Concepts of Moral Theology," in *On Being Responsible*, ed. James M. Gustafson and James T. Laney (New York: Harper and Row, 1968). Haring uses this term to describe what we owe to others.

5. See Ken Collins, *Soul Care: Deliverance and Renewal Through the Christian Life* (Nashville: Abingdon Press, 1995).

6. Dietrich Bonhoeffer, "The Structure of Responsible Life," in *On Being Responsible*, ed. James M. Gustafson and James T. Laney (New York: Harper and Row, 1968). In his discussion of deputyship (responsibility under God), he sees this as one abuse, namely setting up ourselves as an absolute (p. 41 ff.).

7. Ibid. Bonhoeffer sees this as a second abuse, namely, making absolute (and exclusive) responsibility to one person and ignoring all other responsibilities.

8. Richard Swinburne, *Responsibility and Atonement* (Oxford: Clarendon Press, 1989), p. 24.

9. Ibid.

10. Bonhoeffer, op. cit.

11. Bernard Haring, op. cit.

12. See Haring, op. cit. We obviously also play a role in the salvation of others. Thus in the same chapter of Ezekiel noted above, we also find an emphasis on warning others. In warning others of the need to turn from wickedness and to God, we dispense our responsibility and cleanse our own hands.

13. E. L. Mascall, *The Importance of Being Human* (Connecticut: Greenwood Press, 1958), p. 42.

14. Ferdinand Schoeman, *Response, Character and Emotions* (New York: Cambridge University Press, 1987).

15. Clarence Page, "What Help Do We Owe Others?" *Lexington-Herald Leader,* September 2, 1998.

16. Haring, op. cit., p. 105.

17. Swinburne, op. cit.

18. Swinburne, op. cit., p. 123.

Questions for Further Study

1. The author discusses co-responsibility, the idea that our lives are linked and that we owe responsibility to ourselves and each other as well as to God. Do you agree that "We never disobey God and affect only ourselves"? Explain why or why not, giving examples from real life.

2. The author maintains that we become out of balance when we overemphasize any side of the triad of responsibility to God, self and others. As humans, it is always difficult for us to maintain balance. Which side do you tend to emphasize more than the others? Why do you think this is so?

3. What are the dangers of overemphasizing one's responsibility to oneself?

4. Describe the problems caused by over-concentrating on one's responsibility to others.

5. The author says it is possible to overemphasize one's responsibility to God. Do you agree? Why or why not?

6. The author explains that living responsibly before God is acknowledging our life as creatures created by God. Today many public schools teach that we are the products of chance interactions of molecules, not the intentional creations of a loving God. How does this philosophy undermine our society's approach to responsibility?

7. The author illustrates the various ways that meeting our responsibility to God helps us as individuals. Can

you provide more examples of ways obeying God's commands "serves our deepest needs and interests"?

8. Do you agree with the author that some Christians see over-responsibility for others as a virtue instead of a form of irresponsibility? Why would they disagree with the author on this point?

9. Why do some Christians, as the author points out, associate responsibility to the self with sin? Why is self-responsibility necessary for balance in the Christian life?

10. Do you agree with the author that the order of priority for our responsibilities are to God, ourselves, and then others, rather than the more traditional teaching that we are responsible to God, others, and then ourselves? Give reasons for your answer.

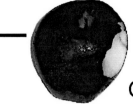

Chapter Four

Choice, Responsibility, and Character

Choice and Responsibility

Making choices forms an essential part of responsibility. In fact, it's pointless to speak about responsibility where choice does not exist. Additionally, one cannot truly speak about responsibility when there is no freedom to choose. Without these two essential ingredients—choice and the freedom to choose—true responsibility is illusory. Choice relates to responsibility in another way: Choice always involves reflection on the decisions for which one is responsible.[1] Ultimately, making wise choices is inextricably linked to the responsible life.

    Evidently God wanted to develop responsible people. That's why he made Adam and Eve free and gave them the capacity to choose. Their freedom is implicit in God's admonition against eating from the tree of the knowledge of good and evil. This warning makes clear that they possessed the capacity to eat or not to eat. God would not choose for them. However, he would clearly set the boundaries and the consequences arising from their choice. Ultimately, the kind of choices we make deeply shape who we become. Godly choices serve to fashion us more keenly into God's image. Ungodly choices set in motion a process of deformation whereby we become more devilish than human.

For what choices are we responsible? What might we learn from the biblical narrative about our legitimate responsibilities? To varying degrees, each possibility appears in the narrative. First, God calls us to choose how we respond to his revealed Word. Second, we must choose how we respond to the environment. Third, we face choices about our internal life. This involves all aspects of our being. However, our discussion will focus on how we grapple with our thoughts and emotions. Finally, we must carefully decide on our actions. By making these choices, we deeply shape our own being and character.

Choices about Revelation

It's abundantly clear that God called Adam and Eve to respond to his revelation in a variety of ways. First, God called them to steward creation and its resources. Thus, we read: "And God blessed them, and God said to them, 'Be fruitful and multiply, and fill the earth and subdue it; and have dominion over the fish of the sea and over the birds of the air and over every living thing that moves upon the earth'" (Genesis 1:28). Second, God forbade them from eating of the tree of the knowledge of good and evil. Again we read: "And the LORD God commanded the man, saying, 'You may freely eat of every tree of the garden; but of the tree of the knowledge of good and evil you shall not eat, for in the day that you eat of it you shall die'" (Genesis 2:16–17).

God freely allowed these neophytes to choose their responses to him. He would not choose for them. They must carefully decide how to react to these divine mandates. What's more, Adam cannot choose for Eve, and she cannot choose for him. Though bound together as one flesh, they maintained their individuality. God did not bring them together in some symbiotic relationship where their individual distinctions were lost. Though they were one, they each maintained his or her unique identity and with it, the capacity to think, emote and choose what to do.

Furthermore, both of them must respond to all of God's mandates. They cannot choose the positive commands and ignore the prohibitions. Both types of commands are binding. Neither can they respond only to the word that comes directly from God. They must also respond to God's word through others. I highlight this fact because Genesis 1:28 indicates that the prohibition regarding the tree was given to Adam. Eve evidently did not directly receive God's word. Rather, she received a transmitted word through Adam. Yet it's abundantly clear that God held Eve as responsible for that word as he held Adam. Both of them bore responsibility regarding the tree.

One must exert great care when speaking about God's word through others. Sometimes others bring a false word carved from their own desires or ignorance. I once heard about a young man, desperate for a bride, who approached more than one young, desirable woman with a presumed word from God: "It's God's will that you marry me." When the first woman did not concur, the young man replicated the supposed word from God to the next desirable female. Just maybe, that word sprang more from his desires than from God's revealed will.

Sometimes, "words from God" spring from greed for gain and carefully planned efforts to deceive. I sometimes wonder about this when certain preachers prey on poor folk for money's sake. Sometimes they stage flamboyant and carefully planned dramatic events designed to play upon the sympathies of the poor. They promise great blessings to those who contribute to God's work. Then they use this painful generosity to line their own pockets.

Nevertheless, it's true that we must respond to God's word through others. This means we must discern carefully, patiently seeking the truth when confronted with a supposed word from God. We dare not casually dismiss the message when someone speaks God's word to us. But we must also avoid being gullible; that is, receiving the word without critical assessment of its truth. We must search it out, discover its truth and, finding it, we must choose to walk in it. We must be like the Bereans described in Acts 17. Unlike the Thessalonians, they did not dismiss God's word. Rather, they received the word with eagerness—but not uninformed acquiescence. They examined the Scriptures daily to test whether these things were really true (Acts 17:11–12). As a result, they believed the truth. Spoken truth became tested truth. Modern Christians should be as discerning and responsive to revelation as these ancient Bereans.

Choices about the Environment

Humans do not live in a vacuum. We live in an environment, surrounded by other people and things. Elements of our surroundings can serve either as a means of enhancing our relationship with God, or leading us away from God. That's true whether our environment is idyllic or painful and harsh.

The latter is an important truth to remember. There's a common fallacy that only harsh environments tempt and destroy persons. Sometime ago I spoke to a church bishop who suggested that people with emotional difficulties come from harsh upbringings. No doubt that's sometimes true. But it's not the whole truth. The famous psychiatrist Alfred Adler knew this. He proposed that pampering as well as neglect can foster maladjustment. He's right. Some of the most maladapted people in our society come from surroundings that ostensibly spelled perfection.

When you get right down to it, it's not simply our environment that poses problems. The choices we make regarding our environment prove to be critical determinants. That's very evident in Genesis. Can you imagine a more idyllic setting? Adam and Eve lived in the Garden of Eden. Eden means "a place of pleasure." It was designed by God for the enjoyment of his creatures. Everything was as perfect as life could ever be. But even there lurked things that could bring them down if they did not choose well, for example, the serpent and the tree of the knowledge of good and evil. They had to decide how they would respond to these features.

That's nearly always the case. We must make decisions about the people and things around us. For example, we must carefully choose our company. We all know that bad company can corrupt even good people. An old proverb says: " A man is known by the company he keeps." The Spanish proverb says it even more directly: "Tell me with whom you walk, and I will tell you who you are."

Sometime ago I read an article titled "What Happened to Jamil?"[2] Jamil was a handsome young man, blessed with a loving family, friends, economic opportunity and a genius IQ. Until he was age thirteen, he was a happy youth. He participated in track and ice hockey and was a good student. After his family moved, Jamil resisted the move and rebelled. He made a number of choices that mystified his parents. He dropped out of school after the tenth grade and became a peddler of stolen guns. By 1995 Jamil had been charged with fourth degree assault, criminal trespass, disorderly conduct, contempt of court and theft. When the story ran, he had been found dead at eighteen years old. He had been shot eight times, his thighbone had been broken, his face cut with a knife. Ironically, this happened after he began to make significant strides in turning his life around. What if he had not made the early choices that he did? What if he had chosen different company? Would his life course have been different? One can only guess. But it's logical to assume that better company would have made a difference. Choices about whom we associate with can make all the difference in the world.

We must also make choices about things around us. Things in our world can impact us negatively. That's true even of good things, which can lead to evil. Money readily comes to mind. In the hands of a wise person, money can be a powerful tool for good. In the hands of the unwise, it may become an instrument of destruction. We often read of Hollywood stars and professional athletes who have made wrong choices about money and brought disaster upon themselves. But it's not just the famous; many average folks make similar harmful choices.

The use of the media and technology also comes to mind. I believe that media can be a good thing. But television and other media have become destructive to some people. The media are used to promote the misuse of sexuality and the exploitation of people. Even innocent children are exploited through things like child pornography.

And what about other forms of technology? It's amazing to sit at your computer and have a seemingly infinite amount of information at your fingertips with just the push of a button. The Internet is an amazing and wonderful tool. But it can also fuel destruction. Internet addiction is a growing problem in our society as people spend days and nights just sitting at a computer terminal, ignoring important people in their lives. They have become slaves to a tool that was meant to serve them. Or think about those who are hooked on Internet gambling or pornography who slowly destroy their lives. These are but a few of the modern things about which we must make choices.

But making choices about how we relate to our environment is nothing new. Even Adam and Eve needed to make choices about their perfect world. Eve needed to make decisions about the serpent and how much heed she would give to this animal. Both Adam and Eve needed to make a choice about the forbidden tree.

Like them, we must make many decisions about our environment. First, we must decide how we will use the things around us. Will we allow them to master us and make us their slaves? Or will we sanctify them to sacred purposes for the benefit of ourselves and others? For example, John Wesley had a famous dictum about using money. He said: "Earn all you can, save all you can, give all you can." The person who maintains a balance among these mandates decreases the likelihood of becoming a slave.

Second, we need to choose the things to which we will expose ourselves. And if we expose ourselves to certain things, how long will that exposure be? Eve may not have been able to totally avoid the serpent. He seemed to have caught her unawares. But she could certainly have limited her exposure, especially when he caused her to question God's word and goodwill.

Third, we must flee or shun some people and things altogether. The Bible gives several examples. Joseph fleeing Potiphar's wife is the first instance that comes to mind. In many quarters today, fleeing a beautiful woman who desires you may seem like the height of folly. But Joseph evidently knew that one cannot take fire into one's bosom and not be burnt. Even more, he knew that to do otherwise would be to sin against God and his master.

In his word to the young man Timothy, Paul admonished: "Avoid such godless chatter, for it will lead people into more and more ungodliness, and their talk will eat its way like gangrene" (2 Timothy 2:16–17). Apparently even talk can be a dangerous thing, eating at one's soul like a cancer. In 1 Thessalonians 5:22, Paul goes so far as to command that one avoid all forms of evil.

Ultimately the reason for diligence regarding the use, exposure and avoidance of some things comes down to the reality of temptation. Things and people in our environments possess the power to tempt us and move us away from serving God. That's clear in the narrative. The serpent became the primary means of tempting Eve away from God's commands. But he didn't do it alone. He succeeded by appealing to Eve's desire for something in her world—the tree and its fruit. He also appealed to Eve's desire to be like God in omniscience, and perhaps even to her physical need to eat. Satan used that ploy with Jesus when he tempted him to turn stones into bread (Matthew 4:1–4). Even legitimate appetites can be misused. Therefore we need constantly to guard our choices concerning our environments.

I need to make one exception to what I have just said. Sometimes the choice about environments may be out of our hands. Most of the time this happens when we don't have the capacity to make a choice. This is most true of children. Some have been abused; they exerted no control over the abuse and were powerless to end it. Such children are not responsible for the abuse or the environment in which it occurred. They did not choose the abuse, even though it deeply shaped them. The damage done to them was not their fault. They need to acknowledge the damage done by others. This may save them from inappropriate self-blame.

However, there's another side to this issue. Sometimes, the specter of abuse may return to disrupt the now-adults' lives in devastating ways. At this point they must make some critical choices: Should they allow those early events to dominate and destroy their lives? Or should they find help within their present environments to begin a process of healing? They must accept responsibility for what they do with their present and their future. This allows the forging of a new future and new patterns of behavior. Of course, some choose to remain in the past, buried under abuse and becoming locked into endless shame and blame that does them no good. At the same time, their backward focus permits the ignoring of responsible choices related to the present and the future.

Choices about the World Within

our env. control and the choices we make regarding the environment shape us

Life is not just about making choices concerning the world around us. We must also make decisions about the world within us. In fact, this involves even more critical choices. Ultimately the world without is not directly under our control, though we can influence it. However, we have a lot to say about the world within us, much more than we sometimes admit. At this point we must exert care in our decisions, for in this hidden, inner world, the battle for sin or righteousness is fought and either won or lost.

Jesus himself highlighted the importance of our inner world. Once, when his disciples were preoccupied with outward ceremonial rituals, Jesus instructed: "For out of the heart come evil thoughts, murder, adultery, fornication, theft, false witness, slander" (Matthew 15:19). He knew how critical the inner world was for shaping our outward behaviors.

↓ inner world shapes our outward behaviors
↓ our theology shapes our ministry

To some extent, the same truth appears in the narrative of the Fall. Eve and Adam must make choices about two aspects of their inner world. First, Eve needed to monitor her mental and cognitive processes. A large part of the serpent's temptation came to her through her thought life. The serpent invited her to think differently about God's command and God's nature. Did he really say that you should not eat of the tree? Was God truly acting in Eve's best interest or was he actually hindering the couple from becoming like him? Once those seeds of doubt were sown in her thought life, she was easy prey.

Second, we must choose our emotions. In the passage, Adam and Eve struggled with shame and fear. Were these the only emotions available to them even after the Fall? Could they have chosen other emotional responses to their sin? Some might argue that these feelings were inevitable. I am not sure about that. In a later chapter, I point out that guilt was a far more appropriate response than shame. Their response partly flowed from their focus. They chose to deny responsibility for their sin and covered it up. Those behaviors are shame's action tendencies. Had they chosen to own up to and confess their wrong, healthful guilt would have resulted. Ultimately, their efforts to avoid responsibility forestalled any possibility for other emotional responses.

Our thought life and our emotions loom large in responsible living. They often serve to shape our behaviors and our character. You may remember the familiar rendering of Proverbs 15:7 in the King James Version: "For as [a man] thinketh in his heart, so is he." The inward thoughts and reckonings reveal the true person. For this reason we must make responsible choices in these areas.

Our thought life is key. Often our thoughts shape our emotions. I often use the following illustration to show how thoughts and interpretations of the world around us shape our emotional life. Let's say a woman who is usually home from work around 6 P.M. is late. In cases where she will be late, she normally calls her family to alert them to the change in routine. Today it's 8 P.M. and she still hasn't arrived and hasn't called. Her husband begins to think: "Perhaps she has had an accident." What kind of emotional response would arise from that thought? Very likely, the husband would feel worry, apprehension, and anxiety. Let's say that after some time, he remembers the fight they had before she left that morning. He begins to think that this departure from the routine is her way of getting back at him. How might his emotional response change in line with that thought? Most likely, he would no longer be preoccupied with worry. He might find himself becoming angry at what he perceives as retaliatory behavior. As he continues to display his anger emotionally and verbally, one of the kids reminds him, "Daddy, tomorrow's your birthday. Perhaps Mommy stopped to get you a birthday present." That thought had never crossed his mind. In his roller coaster emotional ride, he had forgotten that important detail. As he focuses on that thought, he realizes that it has a ring of truth. His anger quickly begins to dissipate and is replaced by happiness and childlike anticipation. He's still a bit frustrated by her not calling but is happy that she remembered his birthday.

Our emotional life is often like that. It hinges on our thoughts and the interpretations we make about our world. By choosing our thoughts, we have much to say about what goes on in our emotions. No wonder that in Philippians 4:8 Paul admonished us to choose our thoughts: "Finally, brethren, whatever is true, whatever is honorable, whatever is just, whatever is pure, whatever is lovely, whatever is gracious, if there is any excellence, if there is anything worthy of praise, think about these things."

choose good things inwardly, in heart and mind

The Question of Control

Not everyone agrees that we can control our internal world. Some fatalistically believe that we cannot help what goes on inside us. They argue that we cannot help what we think or feel. I disagree. Paul evidently thought we could do something about what we think. We can choose the things on which we focus our thoughts. That's the whole premise of cognitive psychology. Cognitive therapists believe that thoughts play a pivotal role in our lives. Moreover, they believe we can do something to change the way we think and on what we focus. Judging from Paul's words, he would largely agree.

I have worked with a great number of people whose negative thought life debilitated them. They suffered from what someone like Albert Ellis might call "stinking thinking." With time, hard work and the help of the Spirit, they were able to move in the direction of thinking more positive things about themselves and their world. They moved in the direction that Paul advised, thereby finding more peace and joy in their lives.

People are more likely to reject the idea of having choice in their emotional lives than in their thought lives. According to some, emotions are outside of our control. Furthermore, these persons argue that since we should not be held responsible for things outside our control, we do not bear responsibility for our emotions.

I do not doubt that people sometimes lose control of their emotions. That's all too clear. They experience an "emotional hijacking." The term refers to those times when we emotionally explode. During these explosions, an area of the limbic brain (the center for emotions) proclaims an emergency. The rest of the brain is recruited to meet the supposed emergency. All of this occurs before the thinking part of the brain realizes what has happened.

The result is an explosion of emotions without out the benefit of any forethought.[3]

But even such cases do not mean that one should not be held accountable. Common sense tells us that persons should bear responsibility for their emotions. Philosophers such as Aristotle believed that persons were responsible for their emotions and passions. Others believe that we should be held responsible for emotions even if we could not help having them. In this way of thinking, simply acting under duress does not diminish one's responsibility.[4]

Some of the latest research on emotional intelligence supports the notion of control of and responsibility for our emotions. Emotions can be trained in both negative and positive directions. People who are easily hijacked by their emotions have unknowingly trained themselves for those responses. For example, instead of exerting control over their anger, they have continually given full vent to their anger. The result can be abusive behavior springing from uncontrolled anger and rage. In therapy, these individuals have to be trained to manage their anger. That's the basis of anger management programs. Angry persons are taught to recognize the cues and triggers to their anger. Over a period of time they learn to choose emotional responses other than anger.

In the same way that one learns inappropriate emotional responses, one can also be taught more adaptive responses. The research on emotional intelligence supports training persons to handle their emotions and passions. Daniel Goleman calls this "schooling the emotions." He notes that emotional learning becomes ingrained through repeated experiences and learning. When these lessons are repeated, ". . . the brain reflects them as strengthened pathways, neural habits to apply in times of duress, frustration and hurt."[5] It's not just our imagination. Practiced emotional life gets hard-wired in the brain.

Apparently the authors of the biblical wisdom literature knew that one's emotions, as well as choices and actions, could be schooled to shape godly character. William
Brown, in his book *Character in Crisis*, highlights how
Proverbs, Ecclesiastes and Job are designed to do just that.
Proverbs has been a source of wisdom and guidance for
me for many years. I have also tried to school my three
sons in the wisdom of Proverbs by building many of our
devotions around it. Many of the principles of emotional
intelligence are laid out in the book of Proverbs.

How do we choose our emotions? We choose negative
emotions when we fail to regulate our emotions appropriately. As a result, we continually give expression to every
emotional impulse without trying to understand what's
going on inside us. Over time that negative way of emot-
ing becomes second nature. On the other hand, as we regulate negative emotions and look for more healthful ways
of responding, we learn to choose positive emotions.

We also choose our emotions when we choose what
we will focus on cognitively. People who focus on only
negative events are likely to experience depression much
of the time. They are like the singers on the old "Hee-Haw"
television show who were always singing about "doom,
despair and agony on me." I once attended a class with a
person I will call Trisha, who said to me, "I can never relax
when things are going right. I keep waiting for things to go
wrong." Not surprisingly, Trisha struggled with depression. Negatively viewing the world and always expecting
catastrophic events nurtured her depressive emotions.

An anonymous author said this about gaining victory
over our emotions and thoughts:

> It will be a sorry day for this world, and for all the people
> in it, when everybody makes his moods his masters, and
> does nothing but what he is inclined to do. The need of
> training the will to the performance of work that is dis-

tasteful; of making the impulses serve, instead of allowing them to rule, the higher reason; of subjugating the moods instead of being subjugated by them, lies at the very foundation of character. It is possible to learn to fix the wandering thought, to compel the reluctant mental energy, to concentrate the power upon the performance of a task to which there is no inclination.[6]

~ yes!

The author is absolutely right. We need not be victims of our moods. We can master them instead of being enslaved by them. Therein lies part of the foundation for godly character.

we can choose emotional response

Choices about Behaviors

Additionally, we must exert care in choosing our actions. Obviously, our choices in relation to revelation, our environment and our internal world influence our actions. For example, our actions reflect a negative response to revelation when we choose to ignore or dismiss a law of God. Sometimes our rebellion against God is also connected to someone or something in our environment. Adam and Eve's rebellion was connected to the serpent and the tree. Those environmental realities became the tools for tempting them away from God.

We dare not ignore the contributions of our internal world. As indicated by Jesus, evil actions such as murder and adultery spring from within persons. It's out of the heart that such behaviors spring. We must therefore exert care in our internal life. No wonder the ancient author of wisdom wrote: "Keep your heart with all vigilance; for from it flow the springs of life" (Proverbs 4:23). That's why people in the Wesleyan camp have insisted that simply changing one's behavior is not enough. More must be done. We must, so to speak, get to the heart of the matter; we need a radical change of heart.

transformation of the heart, not just of outward behaviors

Sometimes we do not understand how these various dynamics relate to our actions. We think our actions "come out of the blue" because we don't understand the hidden motivations or the "schooling" that gave rise to our actions. I was reminded of this by a recent article that described the arrest of a first-grade teacher on a charge of prostitution. From all accounts, this 29-year-old teacher was a well-loved, warm, caring individual. Imagine the disbelief when she was arrested after soliciting sex from an undercover police officer. Apparently this was not an isolated incident as she had been involved in such illicit activity for some time. No one could understand this behavior and neither could the teacher herself. She reportedly said: "I really don't understand what my motivation was. I did all kinds of crazy, disgusting stuff and I don't know why . . . Obviously, I have a problem. It's not every day you find a woman that's married with a child, has a Master's degree and is doing crazy stuff like I was."[7] Whether we understand the bases for our behaviors or not, we are still responsible for the choices we make.

We must choose our behaviors carefully. We will always be confronted with myriad of choices about our actions even in seemingly benign environments. Eve was confronted with action choices—should she listen to the serpent or dismiss him? Should she obey or disobey God? Ultimately the key choice was to eat or not to eat. Similarly after Eve had eaten, Adam faced a choice. Should he listen to his wife and disobey God? Or should he remind her of God's command and choose not to eat? But he too made the wrong choice. He chose to join in his wife's disobedience.

Regardless of the state of our hearts, we are always confronted with such choices. There is no state of grace where we will ever be free from temptations to make evil

þue will always be tempted

choices. Each of us is constantly faced with a myriad of choices between good and evil. Every time we choose evil we make a similar choice more likely the next time. What's more, choosing evil deeds only serves to precipitate a downward plunge and confirms us in evil.

What are the possible behavior choices open to us? We have to make choices about what we will and will not do. A colloquial way of speaking about these choices is to talk about dos and don'ts. Theologians and preachers have spoken about acts of commission and acts of omission. God presented Adam and Eve with choices about things they must and must not do.

These two types of behaviors can be viewed either from the perspective of sin or righteousness. Sins of omission and commission involve a view from negative side. We may also view behaviors from the perspective of righteousness. Then we would speak about righteous acts that one should do and sinful behaviors one should avoid.

Sin and righteousness are polar opposites. To choose one is to avoid the other. Paul makes this clear in Ephesians 4:24–32:

> . . . and put on the new nature, created after the likeness of God in true righteousness and holiness.
>
> Therefore, putting away falsehood, let every one speak the truth with his neighbor, for we are members one of another. Be angry but do not sin; do not let the sun go down on your anger, and give no opportunity to the devil. Let the thief no longer steal, but rather let him labor, doing honest work with his hands, so that he may be able to give to those in need. Let no evil talk come out of your mouths, but only such as is good for edifying, as fits the occasion, that it may impart grace to those who hear. And do not grieve the Holy Spirit of God, in whom you were sealed for the day of redemption. Let all bitterness and wrath and anger and clamor and slander be put away from you, with all

malice, and be kind to one another, tenderhearted, forgiving one another, as God in Christ forgave you.

In this passage, Paul figuratively draws a line of demarcation between sin and righteousness. On one side, he inscribed one act that flows from sin—*lying*. On the other side, he placed the polar opposite pertaining to righteousness—*speaking truth*. As he moved down the page, he filled in the ledger of sin and righteousness: *Sinful use of anger . . . righteous anger; stealing . . . honest labor; evil talk . . . edifying speech*. With each sinful behavior and righteous act, Paul draws the proverbial line in the sand. The choices are mutually exclusive. If one will live as a new creation, the choice is clear. We must choose a firm, consistent walk befitting righteousness.

Some may see this way of thinking as too rigid and legalistic—just another list of dos and don'ts. That's unfortunate! The reality is that we are called to make those kinds of choices if we will follow Christ, not because God wishes to place us in a straitjacket but because he wants to set us free to be all he desires for us. Sin is ultimately slavery and the only way to escape it is to make firm choices for righteousness.

Choice, Responsibility and Character

This brings us to the subject of character. Character is fast becoming a buzzword in our society. Alarmed by escalating violence in our school-aged population, many leaders are beginning to speak about character education. Some school districts across the country are beginning to insist on moral codes of conduct. In Kentucky some have already begun to post the Ten Commandments in their schools and the Kentucky legislature has debated this approach as a way of forming better character in youth.

Defining Character

But just what is character? In *Character in Crisis,* Brown has defined character as involving perception and intention. He also sees character as a way of being that gives rise to a way of acting. For him, character is reflected in the tendency to act, feel and think in certain definable ways.[8]

[margin note: a way of being that gives rise to a way of acting]

In this definition, one can clearly see the link between what we think, emote and do and who we are. Yet the link is not purely linear. Rather, there's mutual influence. Our choices about our thoughts, emotions and actions fundamentally shape our character.

At the same time, character in turn influences our thoughts, emotions and actions. *[margin note: they mutually influence each other]* According to Brown, character and action must ultimately be construed as interdependent referents, in accordance with Henry James's famous dictum: "What is character but the determination of incident? What is incident but the illustration of character?"

Another author has described character as involving badness of desire, badness of belief and weakness of will.[9] Badness of desire involves our proneness to wrongdoing and having desires purely centered on the self. Weakness of will leads to intentionally doing wrong acts. It means that we have little inner resolve that keeps us from doing wrong. It's like having an enemy within that readily sides with every evil desire. Weakness of will is reinforced by badness of belief. This involves having false moral beliefs. It can also involve refusing to acknowledge one's beliefs, to find the consequences of their actions, and, overall, hiding from oneself.[10]

[margin note: 3 diseases of the soul]

These three "diseases of the soul" demonstrate the power of our internal world. They also indicate how critical it is to make appropriate choices about what's within.

They are keys to our character. One also sees here the pivotal role of the environment. Badness of desire, badness
of belief and weakness of will can all be influenced by examples within our environment. Bad examples can serve
to confirm and deepen us in these attitudes of the soul.
      Ultimately, our choices and actions significantly in-
fluence our character and being. One author affirmed
"... we form our characters, by our actions—good acts
lead to good character, bad acts lead to bad character.
The way to forming a saintly character worthy of heaven
is by doing good acts."[11] The famous actress Katharine
Hepburn was once quoted as saying: "To keep your character intact you cannot stoop to filthy acts. It makes it
easier to stoop the next time."[12] How true! Our outward
behaviors certainly influence character.

Choosing to be Devilish

Earlier, I suggested evil choices make us more devilish than
human. Literature abounds with examples of people who
ruined their character by the choices they made. Nathaniel
Hawthorne's *The Scarlet Letter* presents us with such a
demonic transformation. Roger Chillingworth was an eld-
erly husband of a young bride. He had been absent from
his wife Hester Prynne for some time. When he finally arrived in Boston, he discovered that she was on trial for
adultery. A child had also resulted from her infidelity.
Hester is forced to wear a scarlet letter A, yet she refused
to reveal the identity of her lover. Roger became bent on
discovering her lover so he could wreak his vengeance.
      Eventually, he discovered the lover's identity: none
other than the young, revered preacher Arthur Dimmesdale. Under pretence of friendship and providing medical care, Roger, like some hellish imp, preyed on and tormented the unsuspecting Rev. Dimmesdale. But his

choice for vengeance gradually changed him from a calm, meditative scholar to a man with evil deeply imprinted in his visage. Hawthorne provides this apt description of a man becoming a devil:

> In a word, old Roger Chillingworth was a striking evidence of man's faculty of transforming himself into a devil, if he will only, for a reasonable space of time, undertake a devil's office. This unhappy person had effected such a transformation by devoting himself, for seven years, to the constant analysis of a heart full of torture, and deriving his enjoyment thence, and adding fuel to those fiery tortures which he analyzed and gloated over.[13]

Roger didn't seem to realize it, but he was changing himself by his choices. Evidently, one must become a devil if one would perform a devil's office. When we live irresponsibly in relation to God, self and others, we are shaping ourselves. When we fail to make right choices we confirm ourselves in evil. When we fail to do the good, we corrupt our nature and become devilish like him whom we serve.

Another choice is open to us. We can become holy people with God's holy image stamped deep within our nature. That's why God created Adam and Eve with the freedom to choose. He created them innocent. By choosing to follow his lead and make godly choices, they could become the holy people he created them to be. We, too, enabled now by God's prevenient grace, may become creatures of holy character.

Endnotes

1. H. Richard Niebuhr, "On Being Responsible," in *On Being Responsible*, ed. James M. Gustafson and James T. Laney (New York: Harper and Row, 1968).

2. Sarah A. Webster, "What Happened to Jamil," *Lexington-Herald Leader*, January 11, 1998.

3. Daniel Goleman, *Emotional Intelligence* (New York: Bantam Books, 1995).

4. Eugene Schlossberger, *Moral Responsibility and Persons* (Philadelphia: Temple University Press, 1992).

5. Goleman, op. cit., p. 263.

6. Thomas Hanford. ed., *2010 Popular Quotations* (Albany, Ore.: Ages Software, Version 2.0, 1997), p. 25.

7. Tom Lasseter, "First-Grade Teacher at Cassidy Is Charged with Prostitution," *Lexington Herald-Leader*, February 15, 2000.

8. William Brown, *Character in Crisis* (Grand Rapids: Ecrdsmans, 1996), p. 6.

9. Richard Swinburne, *Responsibility and Atonement* (Oxford: Claredon Press, 1989).

10. Ibid.

11. Ibid., p. 131.

12. Katharine Hepburn, *Los Angeles Times* (November 24, 1974).

13. Nathaniel Hawthorne, *The Scarlet Letter* (New York: Alfred A. Knopf, 1992), p. 176.

Questions for Further Study

1. The author says we are responsible for responding to God's word as revealed through others, but that we must exercise great care in discerning God's will this way. Give examples from your life or reading of individuals who were misled and also those who were wisely guided by God's word as revealed to them through other people.

2. Do you agree with the author that "pampering as well as neglect can foster maladjustment" and can lead to a person's making poor life choices? Explain the reasons for your answer.

3. Why do you think Eve and Adam made poor choices, even though they were situated in a fabulous environment?

4. The author says that "we must carefully choose our company. We all know that bad company can corrupt

even good people." How do we balance this obvious truth with Jesus' Great Commandment to take the good news of the Gospel into all the world?

5. What sorts of people or things should we flee or shun altogether, as the author instructs, if we want to live responsibly? Explain your reasoning for each example you give.

6. How can we make good choices about how to deal with traumas from our pasts that were out of our control? Are we held responsible for actions based on situations that were not under our control?

7. Do you agree with the author that we can choose our emotions? Why or why not?

8. What advice would you give a suffering person who feels trapped—or "emotionally highjacked"—by powerful negative emotions?

9. List some concrete steps we can take to avoid becoming victims of our shifting moods.

10. How can we become more aware of the actions we are choosing and the reasons why we are choosing those actions?

11. Which type of behavior are you more likely to find in your life: sins of commission or sins of omission? Why is this so?

12. How can we improve the character of today's children? Adults in society? Ourselves?

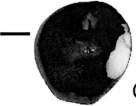

Chapter Five

Five Dimensions of Responsibility

The Five S's of Personhood

What are some of the essential dimensions of our nature revealed in Genesis? Though we could discuss several aspects in the creation account, let's explore five prominent characteristics that loom large in the narrative. These five all begin with the letter S: spiritual, survival, social, sexual and the need for service/significance. God imbedded these characteristics deeply into our nature. We cannot ignore any of them without deeply affecting our lives adversely. At the same time, when we appropriately respond in these areas, we enhance our potential as creatures.

The Spiritual Dimension— A Need for God

Adam and Eve were created as spiritual creatures. God created them for fellowship with himself. This indicates a *spiritual* dimension. According to Genesis, God created us in his image, which explains many things. In *Creation and Fall*, Bonhoeffer emphasizes our freedom and our capacity for rule in creation as the primary dimensions of God's image in humans.[1] Some have pointed to our self-consciousness; others highlight the human capacity for reason and our freedom of will; still others speak of our capacity to create. But whatever else the image of God means, it certainly includes our essential spiritual nature. We are spiritual creatures at the core. We were created to relate to God spiritually. If that area is missing or unattended, our lives become diminished and empty.

In his *Confessions*, Augustine, the Bishop of Hippo from 396 to 430 A.D., captured our essential connection to God and our need for him. Augustine knew well the depth of our spiritual nature. He also knew how impossible it is for humans to extinguish their need for God. For many of his adult years, Augustine lived a reckless, sinful, pleasure-filled life. Today's soap opera characters have nothing on him. All his escapades were vain attempts to satisfy a deep need within himself. In *Confessions*, he writes: " Man is one of your creatures, Lord, and his instinct is to praise you. He bears about him the mark of death, the sign of his own sin, to remind him that you *thwart the proud.* But still, since he is a part of your creation, he wishes to praise you. The thought of you stirs him so deeply that he cannot be content unless he praises you, *because you made us for yourself and our hearts find no peace until they rest in you.*"[2] (emphasis added). Augustine also stated: "So, then I should be null and void and could not exist at all, if you, my God, were not in me. Or is it rather that I should not exist, unless I existed in you? For *all things find in you their origin, their impulse, the centre of their being.*"[3]

[handwritten: we exist because we exist in and through God]

Because we are his creatures, we cannot run from our spiritual selves and be our best selves. If we neglect our connection to God, we impoverish ourselves in the deepest possible sense.

[handwritten: spiritual self: connected to God because we were created, created in His image]

Survival—The Sacredness of Life

God created humans by his very breath for life. We should therefore view life as a divine gift, a sacred thing to be treated with care and a degree of reverence. But God also created us as biological creatures with a capacity for life and all its enjoyment. We possess a zest for life and living—an inherent, human need to survive, to live and to grow. For convenience I call this *survival*. *[handwritten: maybe even to thrive, not just survive]* But in using this term I mean more than simply existing; I mean full, vibrant life, the kind envisioned by Jesus in John 10:10.

I probably don't have to make the case for this strong human desire to live. Never mind that we see suicide in our society. Never mind that there are persons like Jack Kervorkian around. Most of us desire to live. Each year we spend billions of dollars on research to conquer various diseases that diminish life. We spend huge amounts on medical bills when we are ill. Companies institute wellness programs to help prevent and remedy various ills. Many of us are constantly talking about and engaging in programs built around quality of life. The reason for this is because God built into us this zest for life. Those who do not care about their lives diminish themselves. *[handwritten: life is sacred because it was given by God]*

Social—The Need for Human Contact

Likewise, we find that our social nature comes from God himself. He affirmed that it was not good for Adam to be alone (Genesis 2:18), so God created Eve. It took a woman, a human being like himself, to meet this need.

The company of animals could not meet Adam's needs. People need people. God created us this way. We belong to the world of the individual and the world of community. Both of these together constitute being a person.[4] In *The Importance of Being Human*, E. L. Mascall suggests that humans need to live responsibly in community if they would develop and grow as persons.[5] We always stand in need of some human contact to enhance our lives. Bonhoeffer obviously had this in mind when he wrote his classic *Life Together*. For Bonhoeffer, being Christian (and thus what God intended) means balancing individual and social aspects of our lives, balance solitude and community.[6]

Being bereft of needed human contact often diminishes us, sometimes in drastic ways. A few years ago George Hennard, a 35-year-old loner, crashed his pickup through a restaurant window at Luby's Restaurant in Killeen, Texas. He then methodically shot the customers. When he finished twenty-five people, including Hennard, lay dead; another twenty-seven lay bleeding, badly injured. This was the worst killing by a lone gunman in American history. Investigators discovered that Hennard was a walking time bomb; he possessed a seething hatred of people, especially women. Not surprisingly, most of his victims in the restaurant that day were women. Apparently, Hennard hated his mother and the women whose affection he coveted but could not gain. So he became a loner, finding company in isolated fantasies derived from beer, marijuana and music that glamorized violence against women. Hennard reportedly once told his only friend: "I can't make it with people. You're my only friend sometimes."[7] This tragedy represents what can happen when humans, built for relationships, live alone. We become less than God intended, almost bestial, callous to life's sacredness.

Sexual—Intended for Pleasure and Procreation

Also evident in the creation narrative is an unabashed sexuality, another quality inherent to our being. Certainly the sexual act is included in the word about becoming one flesh. It's also partly reflected in a keen appreciation for the human body, something for which we do not need to be ashamed (Genesis 2:25). From the perspective of Genesis, sexuality plays a key part in the enjoyment of life and the propagation of the species. Most Christians have little problem with sexuality's role in procreation. However, they may struggle with sexuality's role in enjoyment of life. That struggle certainly is not the divine intention. The biblical book Song of Songs confronts readers with the pleasurable use of sexuality as God intended.

Hollywood and magazines like *Playboy* have made fortunes from exploiting this side of the human creature. We have built a whole culture around it, much of which misuses and abuses our God-given sexuality. However, no matter how skewed, this intense interest reveals our inherent sexual nature. We cannot misuse and abuse our God-given sexuality without demeaning ourselves. But neither can we run from our sexual selves and remain fully whole.

Noted family therapist Virginia Satir knew the important role sexuality plays in health. She found that most families followed the rule: "Don't enjoy sex—yours or anyone else's—in any form."[8] She also found a depreciating attitude about genitals as necessary nasty objects, things to be kept clean, out of sight and touch. They should be used only when necessary and even then sparingly. Satir continued: "Without exception, every person I have seen with problems in sexual gratification in marriage, or who was arrested for any sexual crime, grew up with these kinds of taboos against sex. I'll go further. Everyone I have seen with any kind of coping problem or emotional illness also grew up with taboos about sex."[9]

From my experience, I have to agree with her. Of course, I would define taboos differently than some, even Satir. Many voices today encourage irresponsible uses of sexuality. These proponents find little wrong with premarital sex and similar extramarital sexual behaviors. They consider anyone who has different views as having taboos. That's not what I mean. By taboos, I mean believing we would be more holy if we were not sexual; such taboos as "sex is dirty" and "sex is only for procreation" demean our status as sexual beings. Remember, God designed you as a sexual creature. You cannot deny your sexuality and be fully whole. At the same time, you must use your sexuality responsibly. From God's perspective, this means using sexuality within the bounds of Christian marriage.

The Fifth S—Service and Significance

A fifth S word, essential to our nature, derives from God's call in Genesis 1:28 to superintend creation. This verse evidently points to the human need to be involved in meaningful work. For some time I struggled to find another S word to express this area. In one of my classes, a student jokingly called this area "sweat." There's a sense in which he was right. Sometimes sweat does connote our life of service. However, much of the time, "sweat" highlights the meaninglessness that is attached to some kinds of work. I am indebted to a student who suggested that "sweat" was all about *service and significance.* God created us to serve and to experience a sense of significance through what we do.

Unfortunately we do not always hold appropriate views of work. In his book *The Fabric of This World*, Lee Hardy has documented some skewed views of work. At one end are those who believe work is demeaning. Work reduces us to the levels of beasts, keeping us from higher activities such as contemplation.[10] From this perspective, work is a curse to be avoided. At the other end of the spectrum, Hardy describes those who believe work makes us gods.[11] We become the ultimate creators and in this sense our own gods. Work becomes an end in itself.

Christians steer a middle ground between these views. Work is not a demeaning activity that reduces us to animals. Work is dignifying. On the other hand, work does not make us gods. Work should not be worshiped for all the trappings of success it can bring. We should see human work as participation in God's work. It provides an opportunity to serve the general good. Alfred Adler, the famous psychiatrist and a contemporary of Sigmund Freud, would call this an expression of *social interest*. From this perspective, the worker understands he is a part of a larger whole and needs to contribute something to the greater good. Work also allows us an opportunity to represent God and steward earth's resources for the benefits of community.

Work in the Christian sense is expressed at two levels. The first is the vertical level, where we offer our service to God. We become aware that whatever we do is an expression of vocation, being called of God (Colossians 3:17; 23–24). From this angle, nothing is mundane. Service becomes a spiritual thing that we gratefully offer to God. However, expressions of service most often take place at the second level—the horizontal. Here we express our love to God through service to family and community and through work. When we serve God through serving others, we experience a sense of significance. Working from this perspective also enhances self-esteem. This partly derives from the sense of participating in something bigger than ourselves, in God's work. This sense of significance may also flow from what one author called *effectance*.[12] Effectance is having the sense that what we do makes a difference, that our behavior produces changes in the world.

Such perspectives fit well the tenets of Adlerian psychology. According to his approach, one of life's significant tasks is work. Failure at work leads to a sense of discouragement for many individuals. This is true because God created us for meaningful involvement in work and to find in it a sense of significance.

Responsibility and the Five S's

Not surprisingly, God's emphasis on responsible living is bound up with these five areas. They form five critical domains in which we must show ourselves responsible. In Genesis, responsibility and the five S's are bound together. We find a similar emphasis in the Ten Commandments (Exodus 20:2–17). God calls us to live responsibly in the areas of the five S's, as shown in the following list.[13]

The Five S's in the Ten Commandments

- *God's exclusive claims*
    1. No other gods, Exodus 20:2–3
    2. No images of God, vv. 4–6
    3. No misuse of God's name, v. 7
- *God's basic institutions*
    1. No work on the seventh day, vv. 8–11
    2. No contempt for the family, v. 12
- *Basic human obligations*
    1. No contempt for human life, v. 13
    2. No contempt for sex, v. 14

- **Basic social obligations**
  1. No contempt for the goods of the community, v. 15
  2. No contempt for the community institutions, v. 16
  3. No lusting after the life or goods of others, v. 17

One clearly sees the spiritual emphasis in the first four commandments. These involve how we relate to God. Basically, God calls us exclusively to relate to him. As such, we should not create gods from that which is not God. Likewise, we should not invoke God's name for our own gain. We should honor God's day of rest.

The survival responsibility primarily comes in commandment six. God calls us to value human life and the integrity of each person. From this commandment, we are called to view human life as sacred. We are to cherish and protect every life. Murder, intentionally depriving another of life, represents the ultimate violation of life's sacredness.

The social responsibilities appear evident in commandments four and eight through ten. This area of responsibilities begins with the family, the foundation of social relationships. However, the latter commandments spread their net to include community goods and institutions. God also calls us to refrain from coveting our neighbor's possessions.

The sexual responsibility comes in commandment seven. God also implies sexuality when he speaks about "coveting our neighbor's wife." The first instance addresses both marital partners. Neither should commit adultery. The latter brings the male primarily into view as lusting after his neighbor's wife. Significantly, God highlights adultery as the ultimate violation of sexuality.

The emphasis on service and significance occurs in several places. Earlier I noted that these emphases find fundamental expression in one's service to one's family, community and work. One finds these emphases in the fourth, fifth, and eighth through tenth commandments.

Some might argue that these are Old Testament commandments, irrelevant to modern Christians. Such persons forget that these commandments, part of God's moral law, are still binding. Moreover, these emphases are repeated again and again across Scripture. They certainly appear in the New Testament. The Sermon on the Mount (Matthew 5–7) stands as a good example. The Sermon on the Mount could be considered the Ten Commandments revisited. One can find spiritual, social, sexual and survival emphases with little trouble. Rather than setting aside these responsibilities, Jesus went beyond them. This appears especially evident in 5:21–48. For example, 5:21–26 expands the meaning of murder; 5:27–32 reinterprets and expands the definition of adultery; 5:33 –37 seems an expansion of the third commandment that involves swearing of oaths; 5:38–42 and 43–48 redefine one's obligations to one's neighbor. Jesus concludes this first chapter of his sermon with an emphasis on love. Evidently, God intended this ethic of love from the very beginning. No wonder Paul wrote:

> Owe no one anything, except to love one another; for he who loves his neighbor has fulfilled the law. The commandments, "You shall not commit adultery, You shall not kill, You shall not steal, You shall not covet," and any other commandment, are summed up in this sentence, "You shall love your neighbor as yourself." Love does no wrong to a neighbor; therefore love is the fulfilling of the law (Romans 13:8–10).

One might also have noticed that the five S's connect to our responsibilities to God, self and others. That is, we show this triad of responsibilities in relation to the five S's. We express responsibility to God, self and others by handling with care our spiritual, social, sexual, and survival needs. We also express responsibility through service, which in turn promotes a sense of significance. These relationships are shown in the following chart.

The triangle inside the circle indicates our three-fold responsibility. We express these responsibilities best by appropriately living out the five dimensions shown outside the circle.

Degrading Human Life

However, when we live irresponsibly in these five areas, we do the greatest damage to human life as God intended it. For example, take the AIDS problem. One can argue that a large part of this disease stemmed from irresponsible living. I do not include here those who were infected through medical blood transfusions, unfaithful spouses and the like. However, when we carve out this innocent group a lot of irresponsible behavior remains. Much of this irresponsibility directly relates to the five S's, especially the misuse of sexuality.

Unfortunately, many in our society tend to use God-given sexuality as a beast-like thing. Many have flaunted their sexuality with every possible partner. A few years ago in the wake of Magic Johnson's revelations, we learned of the escapades of many famous basketball players. Wilt Chamberlain boasted of having slept with over twenty thousand women. This represents irresponsible living to the hilt. In the process, the social fabric of our society has been deeply torn. We have done tremendous damage to our relationships and society in general. How many people have been exploited and used? How many relationships have been fractured by revelations of AIDS status? It's probably impossible to count the cost to relationships stemming from irresponsible use of sexuality.

But spirituality has also been compromised. We have largely negated our spiritual selves through forgetting our spiritual natures. We try to conjure up "spiritual highs" artificially through drugs and one-night stands. Needless to say, such highs bring crashing lows. We have refused to follow God's moral laws, especially those laws that relate to sexuality and fidelity in marital relationships. We have also devalued the sacredness of life, tainting it with drugs and needles that infect our created temples. Some have exploited others through misguided "work" such as peddling drugs and human flesh. We see in these examples the damage to the social, survival and service dimensions of human life.

In Adam and Eve, we can see the damage done in these areas. By failing to respond appropriately to God and his revealed commands, they paid a huge price. They became less than they were created to be in every area. Their spiritual natures certainly suffered, not only in terms of a marred image but also in terms of their relationship to

God. Whereas they apparently once relished fellowship with God, they now cringed in fear. They experienced the horror of being cast out of his presence. They also experienced decreases in their overall quality of life, including their social, sexual, physical being and vocational life.

David: An Illustration of Responsibility and the Five S's

The biblical story of David provides one of the clearest examples of irresponsibility's relation to the five S's. David was a man after God's own heart, but in at least one glaring case David behaved irresponsibly toward God, himself and his neighbors. Three key passages highlight the dynamics of this incident:

1. 2 Samuel 11—David sins with Bathsheba.
2. 2 Samuel 12—God confronts David through Nathan.
3. Psalm 51—David confesses and repents for his failure at responsibility.

In these passages, we discover how failures at responsibility directly relate to the five S's.

- *Service and significance*—David became derelict in his responsibility to go forth with his armies. In turn, this neglect of his obligation provided an occasion for temptation and sexual sin (2 Samuel 11:1–5).
- *Sexual sin with Bathsheba*—This use of his sexuality also involved an abuse of power. It's highly unlikely that Bathsheba had the power necessary to withstand the demands of a king. David used the power of his office to misuse sexually someone with less power.
- *Callousness toward the sacredness of life*—This is most evident in his instigating the murder of Uriah.
- *Social disruption of relationships*—His affair had a number of social ramifications, both private and

public. The passages provide many examples of disruptions in relationship:

1. Bathsheba—David involved her in sexual sin and used his power over her.
2. Uriah—David had him murdered.
3. His own family—David betrayed bonds of trust with his wives and children, impacting their relationship. The social ramifications would long reverberate through his entire family.
4. Joab—David snared Joab by making him an accomplice to murder.
5. David broke his trust with the people of Israel.
6. Spiritual disruption in his relationship with God— David was sufficiently alienated from God to become involved in adultery. He increased the alienation by committing murder and refusing to repent, thus prolonging the alienation from God until Nathan confronted him.

David's adultery in 2 Samuel 11 demonstrates several things about responsibility. First, it clearly shows the five dimensions as key in David's failures at responsibility. When we live responsibly in these five areas, we enhance our lives. When we live irresponsibly, we make a shipwreck of our lives.

Second, it connects failures in these five areas to irresponsibility toward God, self and neighbor. In Psalm 51:4 David laments: "Against thee, thee only, have I sinned, and done that which is evil in thy sight, so that thou art justified in thy sentence and blameless in thy judgment." The verse clearly presents David's understanding of his failure before God. Ultimately, sinful behavior is always committed against God. He is the one who calls us away from sin to live responsible, godly lives.

However, David also sinned against his neighbors. His words in Psalm 51 imply that he wounded only God, which is true in the ultimate sense. But David failed many others. He murdered Uriah; he abused power and trapped Bathsheba into adultery; he sinned against his wives and children. His entire family would forever feel the reverberations of his sins throughout the system. Sexual sins and murder (his two primary sins) would firmly cling to his family. For example, in his children we immediately see sibling incest and rape when son Amnon raped his half-sister Tamar (2 Samuel 13:1–22). In retaliation, David's son Absalom murdered Amnon (2 Samuel 13: 23–29). Later Absalom would conspire against his own father in seeking David's kingdom and his life. As a final act of disdain, Absalom had sex with his father's concubines in the sight of all Israel (2 Samuel 16:21–22).

Finally, David sinned against Israel. Instead of modeling and dispensing justice, he perverted justice. Israel, too, would become caught up in the loss of life that visited David's house. His sins had national ramifications. We are only too familiar with this aspect. In our own time, we saw our nation caught up in turmoil related to President Clinton's sexual exploits. That's the way it always is. The so-called "private sins" of national leaders usually have national consequences and are never really private.

In the process, David failed himself. He failed to live up to his own standards. Here was a man who had once felt guilt because he cut the hem of King Saul's garment (1 Samuel 24:4). At that time Saul pursued him doggedly as some wounded prey. Now David murdered an innocent man with no remorse. He also failed to live up to the honor God bestowed on him. God had called him "a man after his own heart" (1 Samuel 13:14). How unlike that he now appeared! Furthermore, David lost his

saintly, honorable and kingly stature. During this time
of monumental failure, he looked more like the de-
throned Saul.

Third, we see that one irresponsible act can begin a
chain reaction leading to more irresponsible behaviors.
The chapter began with David's first failure at responsibility, his failure to fulfill his kingly duty and lead his
armies in a time of war. But it didn't end there. In quick
succession, we find failures in the other four areas.
Sexual temptation quickly followed with adultery and
murder the eventual outcomes. That's usually the way
it is; rarely do the consequences of irresponsibility remain isolated to one dimension. Usually there is a chain
reaction that spreads to all five dimensions. Because of
this, we should quickly address major failures at responsibility in one domain to stem the spread to other domains. When we don't, we often create an environment
that fuels more severe cases of irresponsibility throughout our lives.

These kinds of consequences evident in David reveal
why God made us for responsibility. Was it to ensure our
failure? No, the opposite is true. Being responsible is the
only way to succeed. It represents the path to wholeness,
growth and maturity. Without responsible engagement
with life we cannot mature as we ought. When God calls
us to act responsibly, he calls us to reach our fullest potential as his creatures.

Thus, by early presenting us with responsible tasks,
God envisioned our enhancement. There is no other way
to grow. Every parent knows that if they allow their children to choose and act irresponsibly, they have a recipe
for failure. Loving parents insist on responsible choices
and behaviors appropriate to a child's age. A loving God
could not create Adam and Eve without an appropriate
call to responsibility.

Endnotes

1. Dietrich Bonhoeffer, *Creation and Fall: A Theological Exposition of Genesis 1–3*, D. S. Bax, trans. (Minneapolis: Fortress Press, 1997).

2. R. S. Pine-Coffin, trans., *Confessions* (Baltimore: Penguin Books, 1961), p. 21.

3. Ibid., p. 22.

4. E. L Mascall, *The Importance of Being Human* (Westport, Conn.: Greenwood Press, 1958), p. 37.

5. Ibid., p. 41.

6. Bonhoeffer, *Life Together*, John W. Doberstein, trans. (New York: Harper and Row, 1954).

7. Madigan, Gonzalez, and Potter, "Gunman Hated Mother, Women—and Himself," *Lexington Herald-Leader*, October 22, 1991, A3.

8. Virginia Satir, *The New Peoplemaking* (Mountain View, Calif.: Science and Behavior Books, Inc., 1988), p. 124.

9. Ibid., p. 125.

10. Lee Hardy, *The Fabric of this World* (Grand Rapids: Wm. B. Eerdmans Publishing Company, 1990). Hardy identifies this perspective with Greek and medieval views, as well as with Freud. In each case, work keeps us from something considered a higher activity—contemplation in Greek and medieval philosophy or pleasure in Freud.

11. Hardy sees the Renaissance and Marxist philosophies as reflecting these views.

12. Everett L. Worthington, *Marriage Counseling* (Downers Grove, Ill.: InterVarsity Press, 1989).

13. Gary L. Ball-Kilbourne, *Get Acquainted with Your Bible* (Nashville: Abingdon: 1993), p. 34. This list was based on the grouping and summary of the commandments found throughout *The Ten Commandments and Humans Rights* by Walter Harrelson (Minneapolis: Fortress Press, 1980).

Questions for Further Study

1. After reading this chapter, you should be very familiar with the five S's, or areas of responsibility. Can you think of any other areas of human responsibility evident from your reading of Genesis? (Your answers don't have to start with the letter S!)

2. What additional evidence can you cite to support the author's contention that we are spiritual beings?

3. The author says that God created us with a desire to survive and to view life as a divine gift. Based on recent news events, is our society's responsibility in this area of survival is increasing or decreasing? Give examples and explain your reasoning.

4. Many of us have very close relationships with our pets. But what do we gain from human relationships that we cannot satisfy with the company of animals?

5. What taboos about sex (if any) did you learn from your family and community as you were growing up? Were these taboos helpful or unhelpful in teaching you to be responsible in this important area?

6. Does your attitude toward your work tend toward viewing work as meaningless labor, or are you more likely to see work as your ticket to the self-sufficient good life? Why do you feel this way?

7. How can work contribute to a feeling of effectance, or having the sense that what we do makes a difference in the world? Are there kinds of work that would not contribute to this feeling?

8. The author says the human need for service and significance is addressed by commandments four, five, and eight through ten of the Ten Commandments. Look at each of these commandments and explain in your own words how this could be true.

9. The author discusses AIDS as an example of damage to human beings caused by irresponsible living. List other current societal problems that are caused by living irresponsibly in one or more of the five S's.

10. Why do you think God inspired the Old Testament writers to tell the full sordid story of David's irresponsible behavior?

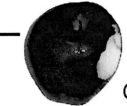

Chapter Six

The Disintegration of the Self

Responsible living enhances life. Irresponsible living diminishes life. This may sound simplified and overstated but it is true. This truth is demonstrated in the Genesis account of Adam and Eve. It is evident that they could have been so much more if they had lived responsibly. For one, they would have moved from mere innocence to holiness by making responsible moral choices. Instead, through irresponsibility, their lives began to fall apart. These are the simple truths of Genesis: Responsibility enhances us but irresponsibility diminishes us. These truths are so universal that we often find them reflected in the themes of the world's great literature.

Victor Hugo's great tale *Les Miserables* showed the enhancement of an individual caused by responsibility. In it, the lead character Jean Valjean, a former petty thief, becomes a man of noble character. His path to responsible living began with an act of grace shown by a bishop. Jean Valjean had been fed by the bishop but repaid the bishop's kindness and hospitality by stealing his silver-ware. Quickly apprehended, Valjean claims the silverware was a gift. The soldiers haul him back to the bishop to check out his story. Not only does the bishop support his story, he also makes Valjean a gift of candlesticks worth two thousand francs.

When everyone has left, the bishop says to him, "And don't forget—don't ever forget that you promise to be a new man." Puzzled, Valjean asks, "Why are you doing this?" The Bishop answers, "Jean Valjean, my brother, you no longer belong to the evil. With this silver I have bought your soul. I have ransomed you from fear and hatred and now I give you back to God."[1]

That responsible act of kindness transformed him. He became a responsible person dealing graciously with God, himself and others. Nine years later he is mayor of a French city. He used his money to buy a brick factory where he had been a laborer. But that's not all! The movie is replete with examples of kindness springing from his new-found responsibility:

- He transforms the brick factory, looking out for the welfare of his workers and ensuring the virtue of the women.
- He rescues Cosette's mother from Inspector Javert even after she spat on him. Later, he tends her as her sickness worsens. As fulfillment of his promise to her, he raises Cosette as her faithful, loving father.
- He uses his money to endow a convent in memory of the Bishop who had redeemed him.
- He arranges a job for the injured Lafite, also buying his horse and cart.
- He reveals his true identity as to save a former prisoner who had been mistakenly identified as Jean Valjean. By this action, he exposes himself to a life-long pursuit by Inspector Javert.

- When he has to flee Vido, he transfers ownership of his brick factory to the employees.
- Once in Paris, he establishes a program for feeding and clothing the poor and hungry of that city.
- He risks his life and is eventually captured by Inspector Javert while trying to save Marius, Cosette's boyfriend. Once captured, he gains Marius's freedom through surrender of himself to Javert. Like the bishop before him, Valjean had redeemed a life. However, the price Valjean pays is much greater than silver. He redeems Marius through giving himself as a sacrifice.

What a transformation! What responsibility he demonstrated toward others! Valjean had fulfilled his promise to the bishop by becoming a new man. His actions toward Javert best exemplify this change. Early in the tale he forgave Javert and kept him in his post as inspector, all the time knowing Javert would continue to pursue him. The greatest evidence of Valjean's change comes at the end when he saves Javert, his relentlessly pursuing enemy, from the revolutionaries. Even after Valjean saved him, Javert promises not to give up the pursuit, and he doesn't. Shortly after, he is on the trail of Valjean again, finally catching him. In the final scene, Javert asks: "Why didn't you kill me?" Valjean replies: "I don't have the right to kill you." Javert continued his query: "Do you hate me?" Jean simply replied: "I don't hate you."

The bishop's words had been realized at several points: Valjean is a new man, more responsible to his neighbors. No longer a petty thief, he becomes a man of noble virtue. Valjean's final words to Javert—"I don't hate you"—fulfilled yet another of the Bishops desires: that he be ransomed from hatred. In the end, he is also ransomed from fear. Javert, moved by the many evidences of Valjean's responsible love, frees him by giving his own life.

Just as literature reflects the enhancement responsible living brings, so it confronts us with irresponsibility's
disintegration. Tolstoy captured this theme in his tragic
tale, *Anna Karenina*. In this dramatic story, Anna eventually commits suicide. It would seem her disintegrative
process began with her illicit relationship with Count
Vronsky. My favorite work reflecting this disintegration
is Oscar Wilde's *The Picture of Dorian Gray*. This is the
quintessential tale of the process of deformation in individuals who live irresponsibly. It reflects in a poignant
way the unraveling of life through irresponsible living.

If you have read the book, you know the evil transfor-
mations that took place in the picture painted of a young,
vibrant, handsome Dorian Gray. Slowly over time the
picture radically changed for the worse, mirroring the
deterioration in Dorian's life. Every irresponsible choice
and act, whether small or great, became mirrored in the
visage of the picture. The picture, you see, was but a reflection of changes in Dorian himself, a mirror showing
the depths of the corruption of his own soul. When he
was cruel to the young Sybil Vane, ultimately contributing to her suicide, the picture changed. A cruelty appeared
in the mouth. So noticeable was the change that he hid
the picture. When he killed Basil Hallward after the latter saw the dramatic changes, the hands in the picture
dripped with blood. Though Dorian remained the same,
every immoral act marred the once beautiful picture.
Slowly over time the picture became a foul, horrific, gruesome thing—something provoking shame and to hide
from others. Like Adam and Eve, Dorian even tries to
hide from himself. He locks the picture away and scru-
pulously guards the privacy of his shameful secret.

In the picture, we see the moral disintegration of the
once honorable and innocent Dorian. Where did this
moral decay begin? The process always seems to begin

with some act of disobedience against God's standards: some failure to respond appropriately to God, self or neighbor. What were these acts of disobedience? Several good candidates appear in the tale.

One could argue that his first failure at responsibility began with his desire to be young forever. That desire represents a clutching at immortality. In many ways it resembles Adam and Eve's original sin, namely a desire to become like God. They wanted to be omniscient like God; he wanted to be eternal. In this way, like Adam and Eve, Dorian forgot his creatureliness. Once we forget our finiteness, we may think and act as though we are our own god, which leads us downhill. We see this truth in the biblical accounts of Nebuchadnezzar (Daniel 4) and Herod (Acts 12:21–23). Both show the slow and sudden destructiveness that comes from believing and acting as our own God.

Or perhaps Dorian's sin grew from heeding the temptations of Lord Henry Wotten. Lord Wotten seems like the original serpent incarnate, a devil disguised as a man of breeding. Dorian irresponsibly followed Wotten's suggestions even though they grated against his own sense of right and wrong. He ignored the warnings of his own conscience and became a slave to Wotten's devilish temptations.

Certainly Dorian's cruelty against Sybil Vane became the first behavioral demonstration of irresponsibility. Following Lord Wotten's advice, he seduces her instead of marrying her. Once he seduces her, he callously breaks the engagement. She eventually commits suicide. Shortly thereafter the cruel tilt to the mouth appears in the picture. At this point Dorian is repulsed by the picture and hides it away.

From this point, it's all downhill, demonstrated in a series of gruesome acts: the murder of Basil, contribution to Allan Campbell's suicide by making him an accomplice in the murder of Basil, debauchery for which he becomes the scorn of London, and the killing of James Vane (Sybil's brother) even though by accident.

In the end Dorian is a broken man who is completely ashamed of his life. By this time he is engaged to Basil's niece, Gladys. Partly to spare her, he decides to leave London. This loving act toward Gladys is, according to Dorian, "his one good deed." But Dorian also wishes to leave to start anew and make amends for his past. Before he leaves, he must destroy the portrait, the telling evidence of a life gone wrong. This represents his last desperate effort to cover and hide his shame. With the same knife with which he killed Basil, he stabs the picture. Alas, he finds that he has mortally wounded himself. Another strange thing happens in his death. Dorian takes on the hideous visage of the picture while the painting returns to its original pristine state. Dorian had been fashioning this outcome his entire life. In every misdeed he was defiling his own soul and body.

The Disintegrative Process in Adam and Eve

This example from literature mirrors similar stories of disintegration found in the Bible, which abounds with tales of people who go off course because they fail to respond appropriately to God. The story of Saul, the first king of Israel, comes to mind. After his failure to obey God in the matter of the Amalekites (1 Samuel 15), Saul begins a slow but sure decline, a descent into a kind of madness, paranoid jealousy of David, many attempts at murder, consulting with witches and finally suicide. David provides an additional example. Following his adultery with Bathsheba and murder of Uriah, David's life also falls apart. He loses his child, his kingdom, his children one by one and his wives. However, David found redemptive grace after making appropriate confession and seeking forgiveness. Unlike Saul, David finally confesses his wrongdoing and finds forgiveness (Psalm 51).

The fall of Adam and Eve provides the first biblical example of disintegration. Perhaps Wilde even had in mind the Genesis narrative when he penned his tale. He endowed Dorian with a pristine innocence mirroring the innocence in Adam and Eve. As Adam and Eve fell under the wiles of the serpent, Dorian fell under the guile of a dangerous tempter, Lord Henry Wotten. Both Dorian and the pair from Eden desperately try to hide their shame. Dorian hides the picture; Adam and Eve try to hide their nakedness, for which they became ashamed. In Dorian we note that the disintegration of his life began with an irresponsible choice and act, a failure to respond appropriately to God, self and others. The same thing happened to Adam and Eve. Like Dorian, their lives also began to unravel.

God created Adam and Eve for responsibility so they would become more than they were. Irresponsibility belittled them and made them less than they were. One sees the ravages of this disintegrative process in the Genesis account. The erosion permeates their entire lives: sensory awareness and knowledge (cognition), emotions (shame and fear), spiritual contact with God, interpersonal relating, body image and sexual relating, and their entire physical being.

The early results of their disobedience are told succinctly in Genesis 3:7: Their eyes are opened; they realize their nakedness; they sew fig leaves; and they make coverings. This rapid reporting implies that the writer of Genesis wants to convey the precipitous nature of the consequences for Adam and Eve. The author also made it clear that these consequences were simultaneous for the couple. They both experienced the results of their eating of the fruit, in direct violation of God's command.[2]

The reference to their eyes being opened points to a change in their sensory awareness and knowledge. But it is not quite what they expected. They believed eating the fruit would lead to increased knowledge, but it doesn't. Instead their eyes opened only to the reality of their own nakedness. They did not gain any new insights into life. The only knowledge they acquired was "A sudden recognition that their nakedness which was wholly proper and comfortable (Genesis 2:25) now was something unpleasant and distasteful. Their nakedness now disturbed them."[3]

The focus on their nakedness also highlights a change in their acceptance of their bodies and their view of sexuality. Their bodies and sexuality, once fully accepted, now become something to promote shame—something to be hidden. Some have taken these details and arrived at mistaken conclusions. For instance, some people have associated the sense of shame with their sexual differences. As a result, they have concluded that the fall into sin consisted of participation in the sexual act.[4] Such a conclusion flies in the face of evidence for the goodness of all creation, including humans with their physical being and sexuality (Genesis 2:25). Nevertheless, it is evident that a sense of shame was awakened in Adam and Eve. Also clear is shame's connection to their disobedience. Shame appeared and brought with it a morbid self-consciousness of their nakedness that was tied to their sense of their disobedience.[5]

In these consequences we see the deceptiveness of temptation and sin. Rarely do we experience what sin promises. Adam and Eve expected to gain new insights and knowledge. But it didn't happen the way they thought it would. Their eyes were opened only to a pained realization of their nakedness.[6] I suspect the same was true of Dorian Gray. He expected to be young forever. Little

did he know that in the end all of sin's scars would become mirrored in his own being, and not just vicariously
in the picture.

Next, we see the beginning of emotional consequences
for Adam and Eve. In the comment about realizing their
nakedness, many authors rightly point back to Genesis
2:25. There they were naked but not ashamed. This new
awareness of their nakedness points to the entry of shame
into their lives. This is not a healthful kind of shame.
Rather it seems to be what some call toxic shame—shame
that highlights one's defectiveness. The eminent Old Testament scholar Von Rad seemed to have this toxic shame
in mind when he noted:

disobedience brings
unhealthy
shame

> For the first time in their shame they detect something
> like a rift that can be traced to the depths of their be-
> ing. Shame always seeks to conceal, it is afraid of "na-
> kedness," and to this degree it can also be given a posi-
> tive evaluation. *But the narrative sees it above all as
> the sign of a grievous disruption which governs the
> whole being of man from the lowest level of his cor-
> poreality*[7] (emphasis added).

But shame is not the only emotional consequence. The
couple hiding from God in Genesis 3:8 points to the fear
factor, which Adam makes explicit in verse 3:10. He tells
God they hid because they were afraid. How quickly
things change. Once God's presence had beckoned them.
Now their disobedience makes that same presence a thing
to fear. From this time, "Fear and shame are henceforth
the incurable stigmata of the fall of man."[8]

Awe also fear in our responsibility because we

Shame and fear often lead to overt problematic behaviors, a sort of behavioral disintegration. In the Genesis account, their shame led to a futile attempt to conceal their actions. Later we find them blaming others
for their personal failure. At the heart of all this is the
defense mechanism we call denial. Denial represents a

must know what we are doing is wrong

refusal to face ourselves, a refusal to "'fess up." The degree of denial often seems related to the degree of shame. The greater the toxic shame, the greater may be the denial. One may be so overcome with shame that the load becomes too heavy. Thus, denial and shifting blame become humans' futile efforts to make life more bearable.

This refusal to accept responsibility may be part of the disintegrative process. That is, the capacity to accept appropriate responsibility may be severely disrupted by continual failures in this area. This may partly explain why some persons persist in denial even in the face of overwhelming evidence to the contrary. They may have eroded their moral integrity and with it the ability to accept responsibility. An extreme form of this erosion may be what was traditionally called "searing of the conscience."

Whether by cover-up or inappropriately blaming others, irresponsible people try to avoid responsibility, mistakenly trying to protect themselves from the "heinous nakedness" of irresponsible behavior. The concealment with fig leaves represented imperfect and inadequate ways that Adam and Eve attempted to hide from themselves and from each other.

We saw the same in Dorian Gray. He hid the picture from himself, keeping it locked away. But he also sought to hide his shame from others. The one man who saw it, Basil Hallward, died for having seen Dorian's shame. Ironically, the man Dorian killed was the very one who had painted it in the first place. Why did Dorian kill Basil? Perhaps for two reasons: because he saw the picture, and because as its creator Basil, more than anyone else, would discern every evil detail resulting from Dorian's sin. Adam and Eve seemed to think similarly. Unlike Dorian, they could not do away with God. Their only resort was to hide from their Creator, who would detect every minute detail of the corruption their disobedience had caused.

One cannot miss the corruption of their spiritual lives. Adam and Eve became morally stained. Spiritually, they now stood deeply alienated from God, cringing in fear of his presence—a presence they once enjoyed. Hiding from God is only the most obvious symptom of a relationship gone wrong. Once they waited with joy for the cool of the day and the opportunity to be with their Creator. Now they feared coming into his presence. Sin always estranges us from God. Thankfully, God still initiates contact. But for his initiating, pursuing love, we would be left to cringe in the darkness of our sins forever.

This rift in their relationship with God points also to interpersonal disruptions. That break is not simply in their relationship with God but also with the self and with others. Hiding their own nakedness from their sight seems a symptom of self-alienation. Aspects of the self, once hallowed, are now considered shame-provoking. For existential and humanistic psychologists like Carl Rogers, humanity's biggest problem is estrangement from the self. Such basic estrangement is thought to flow from two sources: (1) the violation of one's true values to live up to the values of others and (2) the falsifying of one's experiences to conform to the values and expectations of others. I have known people who were strangers to themselves in these senses. They often lost themselves in vain attempts to please others. In this sense Rogers is right. However, that is only part of the story. I have also known people who were estranged from themselves because they had lost the "master plan." Losing touch with God, they lost sight of the larger vision of what they were meant to be. This is self-estrangement of the deepest kind.

Besides the deterioration in their relationship with God and self, their relationship with each other was also affected. Once characterized by innocence and trust, their relationship became marked by pain and domination

(Genesis 3:16). The casting of blame on each other is but the initial sign of the break in their relationship.

Adam and Eve also experienced the erosion of their physical lives. It seems from earlier accounts that Adam and Eve were created free from the ravages we experience in our physical bodies. After their disobedience, they experienced a deterioration of their physical selves. From the context in Genesis we can only assume that childbirth would have been a less painful process. Now it would be accompanied by pain (Genesis 3:16). Additionally, from the time of their fall, their bodies would slowly begin their descent to dust.

They would also experience new problems in their work lives. Adam is told that the ground itself would be affected by their sin. The once pliant and obliging ground would now bring forth thorns and thistles. Adam and Eve also lost their role of service within creation. They were created grounds keepers of creation—a position of leadership and harmony. Now they find themselves in the role of antagonists with nature, living in full disharmony with it (Genesis 3:14–15, 17–18).

In the previous chapter we examined the five broad areas of responsibility: spiritual, social, sexual, survival, and service/significance. Have you noticed that the areas of disintegration discussed above largely fit within those categories? That should not surprise us. When we respond appropriately to God's claims on our lives, we experience enhancement in these areas. When we fail, we begin to experience erosion in these and related areas.

Lessons on Irresponsibility

These examples drawn from literature and the Bible ought to teach us several lessons: First, there is no such thing as a small disobedience or small failures at responsibility. All failures to respond appropriately to God, self and others have the potential to disrupt our lives in major ways. As indicated by the Clinton-Lewinsky scandal of the 1990s, such choices and acts have the potential to disrupt whole nations.

This does not mean that the disintegration is always as pervasive or evident as it was in Dorian Gray or Adam and Eve. Sometimes speedy confession and genuine pleading for forgiveness can short-circuit the beginning of disintegration. However, when irresponsibility persists, disintegration is sure. Sometimes the disintegration in one's life is gradual, occurring over a long period of time. Sometimes the process is precipitous and quick. However it comes, there is always some degree of disintegration, whether visible or invisible.

One piece of evidence that is less visible might be what we used to call the searing of one's conscience; over time continual irresponsible living dulls one's conscience. The conscience loses the sensitivity to judge between right and wrong. In addition, it is no longer disturbed by wrong actions. More visible evidence of disintegration is found in continued addiction to irresponsible behavior. Continual lying that seeks to cover one's actions may be another evidence that disintegration is setting in.

Second, from these examples we learn that the effects of irresponsible choices and behaviors are cumulative and pervasive. Disintegration generally shows itself in all aspect of one's being. No aspect of the self is immune. Irresponsibility is pervasive in another sense. Everyone and everything connected to the one who fails is affected. Thus Adam and Eve's sin has consequences for themselves, for each other and for all of creation.

That's why we must quickly address irresponsible choices and behavior in responsible ways: by confessing and making efforts to repair the damage done. If we don't, we ensure the shredding of our lives and the lives of those around us. Responsible acknowledgment of our sinful choices and behaviors halts or slows disintegration. It's also the starting point of the journey back to responsible living.

Endnotes

[handwritten marginal note: to confess & n' irresponsibility quickly starts process of healing / restoration]

1. Lines are quoted from the movie version of the famous tale. All subsequent quoted lines are from the movie version also.

2. K. Matthews, *New American Commentary: Genesis* Vol. 1A (Nashville: Broadman and Holman, 1996).

3. G. Aalders, *Genesis* (Grand Rapids: Regency Reference Library, Zondervan, 1981), p. 103.

4. Ibid., p. 103.

5. Ibid. The author sees internal guilt as the source of their realization of nakedness and their shame. Given my distinguishing between shame and guilt, I prefer not to use the word *guilt* here, but rather to speak of the sense of disobedience of which they are aware and which they try to cover.

6. Matthews, op. cit., p. 238.

7. Gerhard Von Rad, *Genesis* (Philadelphia: Westminster Press, 1972), p. 91.

8. Ibid.

Questions for Further Study

1. How might Adam and Eve's lives have been different if they had chosen to obey God and refused to eat from the forbidden tree?

2. Contrast the story of Jean Valjean in Victor Hugo's *Les Miserables* with the parable of the unmerciful servant that Jesus tells in Matthew 18:15–35. Although Jean Valjean might have lived to a ripe old age had he chosen not to show mercy, how would he have experienced "disintegration of the self"?

3. Add your own examples to the author's list of literature or films that illustrate how living responsibly enhances life or living irresponsibly diminishes life.

4. In addition to the biblical examples the author cites of Adam and Eve, King Saul and David, list other characters from the Bible who experienced disintegration of their lives because of their failure to respond appropriately to God.

5. How are shame and fear, such as that experienced by Adam and Eve after they sinned, related to each other?

6. What is the difference between healthful shame and "toxic" shame?

7. What evidence do you see in our society that sin alienates people from their loving Creator? How do people attempt to hide from God?

8. Do you agree with the author that there is no such thing as a "small" disobedience to God? Why or why not?

9. Had you ever heard the term "searing of one's conscience" before reading this chapter? Do you agree that this can happen after repeated irresponsible choices?

10. Since we are all sinners, how can we avoid personal disintegration when we behave irresponsibly and sin against God?

Chapter Seven

Excuses, Excuses

Life's All About Finding Reliable Scapegoats!

Humans are notorious for making excuses. We con tinually seek to excuse our faults and failings. We see this truth declared in the play by Irish dramatist and novelist Samuel Becket, *Waiting for Godot*. The play tells the story of two tramps, Vladimir and Estragon. They wait next to a barren, dying tree just outside a forest for one Mr. Godot. Unfortunately, Mr. Godot never comes, but still they continue to wait. Some have suggested that the play borrows from Christian imagery at a number of levels. The barren tree is supposed to conjure up images of the tree of knowledge or the cross. The two tramps evoke memories of humans in their fallen state, and the elusive Mr. Godot is suggested as an image of God for whom they wait.[1] Though Becket denied any Christian imagery, there are several allusions to Christianity in his play. For example, Vladimir made specific

127

references to the thieves who died with Christ, noting that one was saved. In fact, in the dialogue between him and Estragon, Becket highlighted the differences in the Synoptic Gospels on this issue. He noted that just one of the evangelists made reference to a thief being saved; two did not mention any thieves at all, and the third noted that both thieves abused Christ. Vladimir also asked Estragon whether he had read the Bible and whether he remembered the Gospels. Additionally, there are specific references to death, hell and repentance.[2]

These issues aside, Becket made a poignant yet simple statement about making excuses. In the play, Vladimir asked Estragon to put on his boots, which the latter had recently removed. In response, Estragon declared that his boots needed to be aired. Vladimir replied: "There's man all over for you, blaming on his boots the fault of his feet."[3] What a truth! Humans have a knack for excusing anything that reflects badly on them. We will go to great lengths to deflect blame or responsibility from ourselves.

One of my colleagues collects jokes of all sorts. Some time ago he sent me a collection of excuses drivers made to insurance companies. The list reveals the comical lengths to which people go to escape responsibility. Here's a sample:

■ I had been shopping for plants all day and was on my way home. As I reached an intersection a hedge sprang up, obscuring my vision and I did not see the other car.
■ I was on the way to the doctor with rear-end trouble when my universal joint gave way, causing me to have an accident. [Which joint—his own or the car's? Makes you wonder.]
■ As I approached an intersection a sign suddenly appeared in a place where no stop sign had ever

appeared before. I was unable to stop in time to avoid
the accident.

- An invisible car came out of nowhere, struck my car
  and vanished.
- My car was legally parked as it backed into another
  vehicle.

The theme of these excuses is clear. The driver is not
at fault. Something else caused the accident, whether a
fast-growing hedge or a mysteriously appearing sign.
Some of us live our lives like that, constantly searching
for reliable scapegoats.

But we always look for something / somebody to take blame, not ourselves

I saw a good example of this in a Sally Forth cartoon. In the cartoon, Sally's preteen daughter, Hillary,
enters the kitchen. Sally sits at the kitchen table, sip-
ping a cup of coffee and reading the day's paper. Plead-
ingly, Hillary holds up her dripping sneakers and an-
nounces: " My sneakers are soaked." It's obvious what
she wants. Mom should give up her siesta and take care
of Hillary's sneakers. But Sally knows this routine. Without raising her eyes from the paper, she calmly tells her
daughter: "Take the laces out, put the shoes on the rack
in the dryer, turn it on and check them in half an hour."
Hillary begins her whine: "Aw, Mom. That's so much
work." Nonchalantly, Sally replies: "Sorry." Hillary continues her pleading: "But it's not my fault they got wet."
Still calm and undistracted from her paper and coffee,
Sally pointedly retorts: "You took them off, you left them
outside, it rained, and now they're wet. Whose fault does
that make it?" Hillary is about to find another excuse
but her mom quickly cuts her off with the words: "The
statute of limitations has run out on El Niño." Reluc-
tantly, Hillary leaves to care for the sneakers. When we
next see her, she is angrily placing her shoes in the dryer
and thinking to herself, "The trouble with life is there
aren't enough reliable scapegoats."[4]

Does that ring a bell? I am not simply speaking about the antics of kids. Many adults pull the same routine for far more serious behaviors than getting shoes wet. Sometimes we seek scapegoats to explain our sinful choices and behaviors. Often the scapegoats are those closest to us: our parents, siblings, partners, or children. Anyone is fair game as long as we can deflect responsibility from ourselves.

This doesn't mean that some persons have not been victimized. Neither does it mean that others are always guiltless. Sometimes other people may have hurt us and done us grave wrong. But even then, while acknowledging those wrongs, we must take responsibility for our present choices and behavior. To do otherwise means becoming hopelessly trapped in our pain and predicaments, whatever they may be.

Our society seems to be encouraging this finding of reliable scapegoats. We often promote a culture of victimhood. This cultural mindset perceives individual problems as springing from one's being victimized in some way. These victims can then blame every misdeed on someone else. Ultimately we get the idea that we are not responsible for our deeds; someone or something must carry the blame. This tendency to find good scapegoats to cover guilty culprits is evident in many sections of our society. It's endemic to our legal and judicial systems. We sometimes find the same propensity within the mental health community. Sometimes we are all too ready to blame present faults on a person or event from the past.

This search for scapegoats runs deep. When human scapegoats aren't readily available, we turn to the next available warm-bodied thing, such as a dog or a cat. Thus the proverbial excuse made by many a negligent school kid: "The dog ate my homework."

When no animal is available, we may resort to blaming inanimate objects—such as Estragon's blaming his boots. Of course, enhanced technology provides us with a whole new set of scapegoats. Today's techno kids are likely to blame their failure to complete homework on malfunctioning computers.

When the natural realm fails to provide an appropriate sacrificial lamb, we turn to the supernatural. "I couldn't help it. It was in the stars," we might declare. Or as comedian Flip Wilson used to say: "The Devil made me do it." Of course there's some slight truth to that assertion. The Devil certainly does tempt us. But we use that excuse to deny our choice in cooperating with the Devil. When all else fails we may even resort to blaming God. Adam evidently meant to do this when he told God: "The woman whom thou gavest to be with me, she gave me fruit of the tree, and I ate" (Genesis 3:12).

How did we get this way? The Genesis account suggests that excuse making is deeply rooted in our earliest history as human beings. We resort to making excuses whenever we are in danger of compromising ourselves. This tendency is so ingrained that it might appear to spring from some flawed gene passed down from Adam. Of course, it's not really a problem of our genes. Rather, excuse making is a matter of personal choice. We choose to make excuses rather than squarely face responsibility for our decisions and actions.

Making excuses comes so naturally that for many of us it becomes an automatic response, like a knee-jerk reaction. The reaction is so quick that the excuse is already made before our minds can adequately evaluate its truth and censor our words. Sometimes we are so busy creating excuses that we engage in misspeak. When asked about his marijuana use, President Clinton confessed to using the drug but tried to give himself a way out by

misspeaking: "I didn't inhale." How laughable! Not surprisingly, that line became the butt of jokes in many a
late night talk show. Excuses are quick, automatic but
don't necessarily make sense.

The Great Cover-up

By definition, an excuse is an attempt to shield the self
from accusations. One gets this sense from the etymol-
ogy of the word. Excuse comes from the Latin word
excusare, a combination of *ex* (from) and *causa* (accusation). Making an excuse is a method that seeks to remove
blame from the self by deflecting it onto some other ob-
ject. Excuses are means of avoiding exposure of a personal fault, omission or sin. In this sense, excuses serve
as a kind of psychological covering shielding the self from
nakedness before others.

In the Genesis account, Adam and Eve really try to
cover up their sense of shame in two ways. The most obvious is their feeble attempt to cover their physical bodies with piecemeal garments of fig leaves. Of course the
fig leaves failed to cover their nakedness and their shame
adequately. Such cover-ups always fail.

However, we can become focused on this attempt at
physical covering and miss their second effort to cover
their failure, sin and shame. Sin and shame are not tan-
gible realities easily covered with things like fig leaves,
so one must double one's efforts and use all the means
at one's disposal to cover the inner self. One must resort to evasive words and psychological gyrations to con-
vince the self that one is clothed when in reality one is
stark naked. Excuses are the verbal equivalent of physical fig leaves. The purpose is the same, to cover up something. Ultimately, this strategy is just as ineffective as
are the leaves.

Nevertheless, these mental and psychological gyrations have power, although not the kind we desire. The old story of the emperor's new clothes provides humorous testimony to their power. Excuses have real power, namely the power to delude. We may excuse ourselves for so long that after a while we come to believe the myth we have created.

Why all this effort to cover up? It's because the pain from spiritual and psychological wounds is just as real as the pain from physical injury. It's like having our flesh split open, revealing sinews and bones and leaving us with gaping, bleeding wounds. In fact, some would argue that the pain from sin or shame is much more excruciating. Those wounds go much deeper than body tissue. They sear us at the very depths of our souls. Sometimes those wounds remain long after physical wounds have healed.

Trauma situations reveal how deeply nonphysical wounds can go. I am not suggesting that trauma necessarily derives from personal sin; I am merely trying to show that wounds of the spirit and mind go deep. Consider a person who lived through a car wreck where there was a real possibility of losing his or her life. Let's also suppose that this person sustained many physical wounds in the wreck. Over time physical wounds usually heal. However, the psychological wounds may persist long after physical injuries have healed. The individual might fear driving or being in a car. To protect the self, that individual might even avoid all contact with cars. In this case, the avoidance is a covering, a protection from exposing the self to the traumatizing situation and exposing one's fear and pain.

Problems rooted in our spirit and sense of sin need covering just as much as physical wounds need bandages. Deep down we all know that. So the problem is not so much that we use covering but that we use the wrong covering.

instead of confession,
confession, restoration and
healing by God

Often, we try to cover this sense of failure and shame with psychological garments like excuses, denial and rationalization. We may also cover ourselves by avoiding anything that reminds us of our real state. Adam and Eve used all of these methods to some extent, not only making excuses, but avoiding God. Such efforts are rarely adequate even though we persist in them. We sometimes see through our own vain psychological efforts to cover ourselves. When it's all said and done, the results are the same as if we had used flimsy leaves. We are still naked.

The Ultimate Motive: Self-Protection

At the risk of overstating myself, I suggest that excuses are always meant to cover the self—to protect something about the self. Usually we are not only trying to avoid culpability, we also seek to protect ourselves from something. Much of the time excuses are intended to protect us from overwhelming negative emotions like shame and guilt. Someone I know once told me: "If I accepted all the responsibility for all the things I have done, it would be too overwhelming." To protect himself, he covered himself by continually making excuses. All the time, at some level he knew that this was an illusory garment, very much like the Emperor's new clothes. He deluded himself into thinking that his excuses actually covered his irresponsibility. But as revealed in his statement, he knew it didn't, although making the excuse momentarily helped to protect him from overwhelming guilt.

Even when we excuse others we are really trying to protect ourselves. Often individuals who persist in making excuses for their family are trying to protect some image of the family. Losing that image represents some loss to the self. In this sense, they are protecting themselves from what they perceive as a personal loss.

I once worked with someone whom I will call Jane. Jane always made excuses for her mother. She found it difficult to hold her mother accountable for any of her past behaviors. She took the opposite stance to what we sometimes see in counseling, blaming one's parents for everything. She excused her mother for every behavior—neglect, inconsistent modeling, sinful behavior and other things that she called "Mom's mistakes." Surprisingly, she found it easier to blame some of her older siblings for not being there for her while excusing her mom for even more extreme examples of neglect. I found this surprising. Normally one expects that a mother should be held more accountable for spending time with a child. This business of making excuses for mom became a continuing theme during the counseling sessions. I once asked Jane, "What would it mean for you if you stopped making excuses for your mom?" After a thoughtful silence, Jane said, "Then I would have to face the fact that I wasn't as important to mom as other people were." Making excuses for her mom shielded her from feelings of being unloved by the person whose love she most needed.

In his book *Taking Responsibility*, Nathaniel Branden provides another example of this phenomenon. Branden relates the story of Eric, one of his former clients. According to the author, Eric was "shy, rigid, socially inhibited, with the appearance of being emotionally tortured." Yet Eric described his parents as warm and loving and his childhood as an ideal one. Through hypnosis a far different picture emerged. He had in fact endured for many years physical abuse from his father and continuous ridicule from his mother. What was he gaining from the fictional narrative of an idyllic childhood? How was he protecting himself by making excuses for his parents? In a later session Eric came to a remarkable conclusion:

If I were willing to be responsible for my own life, if I didn't believe I somehow needed my parents' support for my survival—I don't mean financially, I mean *spiritually*—I could look at my childhood and see it for what it was.[5]

Apparently, Eric depended on his parents for his psychological survival. Thus he created an elaborate tale of their love and nurture. By maintaining a fictional image of his parents, Eric was really protecting his own need for survival. However, it also appeared that this effort shielded him from assuming primary responsibility for his own life.

These examples provide insight into excuse making: When one sees individuals persistently making excuses for others, one should ask: "What illusion is the individual protecting?" "From what hurt or pain is the individual protecting the self?" "What parts of the self are especially vulnerable and need protecting?" "What secondary gains does one derive from making excuses?" Excuse making, at its core, is really about protecting the self, even when ostensibly done to excuse others.

The Paradox of Excuse Making

Unfortunately making excuses rarely achieves its purpose. Thus, we are not surprised that Adam and Eve's ploys don't work. Their attempt at covering their shame and nakedness through leaves is woefully inadequate. God must later provide for them a more appropriate covering of skins. Neither does the psychological covering sewn together with excuses work. God sees behind their excuses and still pronounces them guilty.

In fact, excuses often make matters worse. Shakespeare was right when in *King John* he places on the lips of Pembroke the following words:

And oftentimes excusing of a fault
Doth make the fault the worse by the excuse:
As patches set upon a little breach
Discredit more in hiding of the fault
Than did the fault before it was so patch'd.[6]

How do excuses make matters worse? First, making excuses has the power to create deep rifts between persons. We see this in the Genesis account. Adam blames Eve and Eve blames Adam. Then to protect themselves, they each begin to rat on the other. The Genesis scene creates a picture in one's mind of two persons whose excuses have created a deep rift between them.

Second, making excuses also has personal consequences that work to the individual's detriment. In a sense, making excuses is an exercise in self-delusion. It shuts off personal awareness of one's true condition. It allows one to ignore reality. This can be embarrassing or even dangerous. Remember the story of the emperor's new clothes. His exercise in self-delusion led to a very embarrassing moment when the observant boy yelled: "The emperor's naked!" Perhaps it would not be such a great problem if embarrassment were always the only consequence. But in Adam and Eve's case the consequences were more dire—the possibility of being eternally stuck in their sin.

Returning to the metaphor of using excuses as a covering might help explain what I mean. Excuses may cover one's wound and thereby hinder the individual from seeking true healing. In this sense, making excuses can sometimes place insurmountable barriers to one's healing in all realms—physical, psychological or spiritual. In the Genesis narrative there is a noticeable lack of appropriate guilt for their sin. Rather, one finds only shame and fear and excuses designed to cover their transgression. One wonders if their excuses cut them off from a healthful guilt response. They had convinced themselves that it wasn't really their fault and they felt no remorse. What they needed was a good dose of guilt to get them back on track.

Excuses not only hinder guilt and repentance, they also hinder development of the self. That is, excuses create barriers to becoming the mature, growing individuals we were created to be. They stunt our growth and diminish us. Growing individuals are those who appropriately take responsibility for their choices and actions. As Sydney Harris reminds us in *On the Contrary:* "We have not passed that subtle line between childhood and adulthood until we move from the passive voice to the active voice—that is, until we have stopped saying 'It got lost,' and say, 'I lost it.'[7] Saying something "got lost" is an attempt to shift responsibility. Saying "I lost it" is the sign of a maturing, responsible individual.

As you might have realized by now, there's a paradox in making excuses. We normally intend excuses to protect us from a perceived threat, harm or loss. In reality, when we make excuses, we actually hurt ourselves. Rather than lightening our burdens, excuses tend to add to them. We often become stuck with our burdens because excuses rarely provide the anticipated relief.

Finding Healing: Getting Beyond Excuses

To find healing and relief, we must get beyond our excuses. We must come to the place where we own our part in our varied predicaments and become responsible for our choices and behaviors rather than shifting blame on other people or things. Furthermore, those who care must help irresponsible persons to become responsible

[handwritten margin note: Allow no excuses for yourself or others]

individuals. We must allow no excuses. At first glance, not allowing excuses seems like a callous, uncaring response. In fact, it is really the only redemptive response. Only through taking appropriate responsibility will one experience healing.

One finds this explicit emphasis on allowing no excuses in William Glasser's *Reality Therapy*. Glasser believes that in order to help clients, therapists must eliminate the use of excuses from the lives of clients. Correspondingly, the therapist must help clients to take responsibility for their choices and behaviors.[8] Excuse making (another name for irresponsibility) and responsibility are polar opposites. They cannot exist together. The combination of not making excuses on the one hand and taking appropriate responsibility on the other helps to bring healing into a person's life.

[handwritten margin note: Responsibility brings healing, excuses do not, though they may have temporary relief]

In these two emphases, Glasser is right. Recovery and healing come only when there is appropriate responsibility. Earlier I spoke about making excuses as a form of cover-up. To follow through with that metaphor, we may think about taking responsibility as a form of uncovering. When we take responsibility we uncover our sin and bring our wrong choices to the light. This uncovering (another name for confession) helps the healing to begin.

[handwritten margin note: Confession is a responsibility, to return to God and say. I messed up]

Sometimes persons take responsibility for their choices and actions on their own without any outside pressure. Such persons have moved from the passive voice to the active voice. They have quit saying, "It got lost" and now say, "I lost it." That's a sign of a maturing individual, a person on the mend who is well on the way to healing and redemption.

However, sometimes our denial and rationalization are so deeply rooted that someone must press us into a corner for us to accept responsibility. That seems to be the case in the Genesis narrative. Adam and Eve are deeply entrenched in a pattern that shifts blame and avoids responsibility. God must confront them and press them until there is no escape from their irresponsible choice.

Some features of the Genesis narrative remind me of an intervention that's often done with alcoholics, who are notorious for excuses, rationalization and denial. They don't take responsibility for their habit very well. The intervention is intended to confront alcoholics with their behaviors so as to break through the deep denial. In this intervention, significant persons in the alcoholic's life collect "the goods" on the alcoholic. Those persons may include a spouse, children, friends, or an employer. Over a period of time they collect evidence on the alcohol problem and its consequences. At a designated time and place, the alcoholic is confronted with the evidence from all these sources. Every effort to avoid responsibility is met with new data from a source that allows the alcoholic no escape. If this is successful, it has the effect of breaking through the denial and opening the door to help.

God seems to be doing something like this in the Genesis passage. The difference is that God is the one source who has all the evidence necessary to convict Adam and Eve and bring them to responsibly owning their sin. God took the same approach when he had Nathan confront David regarding his sin with Bathsheba. And for what purpose does God do this? Not to condemn alone, but ultimately to redeem and heal.

Endnotes

1. Wallace Fowlie. A synopsis and analysis of the play by Samuel Becket, originally published in *Dionysus in Paris* (New York: Meridian Books). Retrieved from the World Wide Web on March 23, 2005.

2. Samuel Becket, *Waiting for Godot: Tragicomedy in Two Acts,* Act 1 (New York: Grove Press, 1954).

3. Ibid., p. 8.

4. Greg Howard, "Sally Forth," *Lexington Herald-Leader,* July 5, 1994.

5. Branden, Nathaniel, Taking Responsibility (New York: Fireside, 1996), p. 129.

6. William Shakespeare, *King John,* act 4, sc. 2, lines 30–34.

7. Sydney J. Harris, *On the Contrary* (Cambridge, Mass.: Riverside Press, 1962), pp. 290–291.

8. See William Glasser, *Reality Therapy: A New Approach to Psychiatry* (New York: Harper and Row, 1965); and William Glasser, *Control Theory* (New York: HarperCollins, 1989).

Questions for Further Study

1. Can you supply any further examples from literature, television programs or films—either humorous or serious—of outrageous attempts to shift blame to other people or even inanimate objects?

2. Why do we often choose scapegoats for our irresponsibility from those who are closest to us, such as our parents, siblings, partners, or children?

3. What is the difference between a scapegoat and a legitimate reason for doing something wrong? Is it easy or hard to tell the difference? Listing examples of each may help you decide.

4. Do you agree with the author that we cannot blame the Devil for our sins? Explain your answer.

5. If excuses are the wrong covering for our sin and shame, what is the proper covering for our spiritual wounds?

6. Why do we sometimes attempt to protect ourselves by making excuses for others?

7. What is the "paradox of excuse making" the author describes?

8. In what ways do excuses make matters worse than they already are?

9. Why does the author say a good dose of guilt would have helped Adam and Eve?

10. Do you agree with the author that we should never allow excuses in ourselves or others? Why or why not?

Chapter Eight

Shame and Responsibility

Barometers of the Spiritual Life

[handwritten: emotions as spiritual barometers?]

Emotions are spiritual barometers. They often reflect positive or negative shifts in our spiritual lives. When we live responsibly, we generally experience positive emotions such as joy and contentment. When we live irresponsibly, a jangled complex of negative emotions may ensue, such as embarrassment, shame and guilt.

This truth is evident in the Genesis account of the Fall. Following their sin, Adam and Eve become painfully aware of a shift within their lives. What's more, that shift is largely described in emotional language. The first emotion is explicitly named within the context: they became fearful. The second is inferred from a previous statement. In Genesis 2:25, Adam and Eve were naked but not ashamed. Now they became morbidly aware of their nakedness. Concomitantly, they experienced an unwholesome sense of standing before God fully exposed and

[handwritten: experience fear and shame after sin]

143

vulnerable. As a result, they attempted to cover their nakedness. Adam and Eve had lost their sense of unashamed
innocence and in its place experienced what some might
call toxic shame. In his book *Shame: The Exposed Self*,
Michael Lewis sees their attempts to cover and hide as
shame behaviors. For him shame is the central emotion
and the focus of attention in the narrative.[1]

This negative shift in emotions in Adam and Eve after their disobedience represented a drastic change from
innocence to shame. Joyous fellowship once characterized their contact with God, but they found themselves
hiding from him in fear. That's why emotions are spiritual barometers. Emotions such as joy suggest health in
one's spiritual life. On the other hand, negative emotions
such as fear, shame and guilt suggest that something has
gone awry. In this sense, negative emotions serve a function akin to the part played by pain in the physical body.
Our pain receptors tell us that something is wrong in our
physical body. If we are wise, we seek medical help to
address the problem. The same is true of negative emotions. They can tell us something is vitally wrong within
our spiritual or psychological lives. Some emotions such
as guilt can lead us to take reparative steps if we listen to
what that guilt is saying. Others like shame and fear may
freeze us in our tracks. Rather than leading us to seek
repair, they may lead us to avoid or cover up our true
spiritual state.

That's why Christians ought not to downplay the role
of emotions. God created us for emotional life. And as
indicated above, much of the time emotional realities are
integrally tied to spiritual realities. In the Genesis account, those spiritual realities include willful sin and a
subsequent desire to avoid God.

This connection between emotional response and
spiritual realities doesn't occur only in the first chapters

of Genesis. We find the pattern throughout the Bible, especially in places like the psalms. For example, in Psalm 32:10–11, out of his own experience, David wrote: "Many are the pangs of the wicked; but steadfast love surrounds him who trusts in the LORD. Be glad in the LORD, and rejoice, O righteous, and shout for joy, all you upright in heart!" David is obviously making a connection between sorrow and wickedness. In contrast, he sees joy as the heritage of those who are upright in heart. In Psalm 51:12, David sees the loss of joy as a direct result of his sin with Bathsheba: "Fill me with joy and gladness; Let the bones which thou hast broken rejoice." Later in the psalm he wrote: "Restore to me the joy of thy salvation, and uphold me with a willing spirit" (v. 12).

It's significant that the writer of Genesis focuses on the emotions of fear and shame. In that context, they mirror each other on two levels. Shame represents disruptions on the horizontal level—within and between persons. Fear represents something gone horribly wrong on the vertical level, namely in Adam and Eve's relationship with God. But that's not all! Shame and fear share other features: They both seek to conceal, to estrange, and to avoid personal responsibility for deeds done. I shall say more about these aspects when I discuss the nature of shame. That doesn't mean that one should dismiss fear. I have simply chosen to focus on shame, since it appears as the most central emotion.

Shame—A Failure at Responsibility

What is the source of shame? The biblical narrative provides some answers. Some commentators suggest that sexuality served as the basis for shame in the Genesis passage.[2] This doesn't quite fit the Genesis account. Granted, misuse of our sexuality may contribute to the presence of shame within our lives. Some of the world's great literature portrays ways the improper use of sexuality can result in painful shame. That's evident in Tolstoy's *Anna Karenina*. The heroine, Anna, and her lover, Count Vronsky, suffer a deep sense of shame from their illicit love. Following their first intercourse, Tolstoy writes: "There was something horrible and revolting in the memory of what had been bought at this fearful price of shame. The shame in the presence of their physical nakedness crushed her and took hold of him."[3] We see a similar theme in Gustave Flaubert's *Madame Bovary* and Nathaniel Hawthorne's *The Scarlet Letter*. In all three works, shame sprang from the improper use of sexuality.

However, sexuality as understood in the Bible is a good thing. It is one of the aspects of creation that God pronounced good. Sexuality per se is not a basis for shame. We may infer this from Genesis 2:25. There we read that the couple were naked but were not ashamed. Adam Clarke, commenting on that passage, noted: "And as sin had not yet entered into the world, and no part of the human body had been put to any improper use, therefore there was no shame, for shame can only arise from a consciousness of sinful or irregular conduct."[4] Thus, it seems illogical to assume that it is sexuality that now brings them shame. Something new had entered their experience to bring about this emotion and foster their need to cover themselves. Adam and Eve had become morbidly self-conscious. They felt totally exposed. What made for this fear of exposure even to an intimate other? The context suggests that disobedience to God was the one thing that could have brought about this experience. They had violated the clear standard God had laid out for them.

Michael Lewis gives some insight into the basis for shame in the Fall narrative. In Lewis's model, shame is produced by the mixture of two essential ingredients. The

first is the capacity for self-awareness. **Second,** shame requires awareness of internal and/or external laws governing behavior.[5] In the Genesis account, the law to be kept is the prohibition regarding eating from the tree. The coupling of their awareness of the standard and the violation of it produced their sense of exposure. *they had to know*

Significantly, early Renaissance painter Masaccio's *the shadow* fresco titled "Expulsion from Paradise" was chosen as the *muscle was,* cover for Lewis's book *Shame: The Exposed Self.* In this *they chose to disobey* masterpiece, the original couple demonstrates the deep pain and shame from their deed. Both are cast from the garden naked except for leaves that provide insufficient cover. Eve's right hand covers her breasts while her left hand assists the sparse leaves covering her genital area. Her eyes are closed and her open mouth seems to utter a silent scream. Adam, overwhelmed with shame, buries his head in both hands. It's a very moving and revealing piece that captures the shame and pain Adam and Eve must have felt at their fall from grace and their subsequent expulsion from Paradise.

Of course, Christians know something that Masaccio omits from his painting: although they are expelled from Paradise, the couple also experienced God's grace. Masaccio shows them clothed with leaves while the Bible tells us that God considered their sense of shame and exposure and graciously provided more adequate clothing. In the slaying of animals to obtain skins for their clothing, one assumes that God provided a means of atonement. But in this act he also covered them from physical and perhaps psychological exposure.

Choices that Shame Us

But why did Adam and Eve fail to respond appropriately to God by heeding his standards? We can glean several possible answers from the Genesis narrative. First, we often fail to heed God's standards because we listen more intently to other voices. Often, those "other voices" advocate standards far different from God's. In our day, those voices include the voice of political correctness and tolerance at all costs. Often those modern standards suggest that biblical values are naïve, outdated and judgmental. One prominent example lies in the area of sexuality. Sometimes professing Christians ignore God's Word against premarital sex and adultery. Desiring the world's approval and hesitant to be labeled intolerant or bigoted, we often capitulate to the world's definitions of what is right and wrong.

This was prominently illustrated for me a few years ago when I read some figures from a poll of Christian teenagers conducted by Bill Bright's organization. I was shocked to learn that well over 60 percent had been involved in premarital sexual activity while professing Christian beliefs. It seems that these were people who professed one thing but did another. Knowing teenagers, I suspect that the "other voices" were those of their peers who consider remaining a virgin uncool.

The other voice in the Genesis text is the voice of the serpent. He casts suspicion on God's commands. Rather than intending these commands for humanity's good, the serpent hisses, they spring from God's envy of humanity's possibilities. Of course, this is a rather preposterous theory considering the creaturely nature of humans! Why would God be envious of his creatures? In what ways could these limited creatures match the level of their omnipotent Maker? But Adam and Eve believed the serpent. This illustrates a sad reality: When we listen to other voices above God's voice, sound reasoning often goes out the door.

In addition to our choosing to listen to voices other than God, a second implied reason for violating God's

[handwritten marginal note: that we are in control and know best]

standard is our tendency to think that we know better than God. We prefer our private opinions about God above his clearly revealed Word, and end up following our own ways rather than God's. Noted biblical commentator Gerhard Von Rad sees this attitude as the oldest of human flaws. He noted: "Man's ancient folly is in thinking he can understand God better from his freely assumed standpoint and from his notion of God than he can if he would subject himself to [God's] Word."[6]

In this attitude, Adam and Eve remind me of certain teenagers. Teenagers also tend to think that they know much more than their parents. They consider their parents too old-fashioned, too strict, too out of touch with the modern world to be heeded. What do parents know anyhow? This attitude reflects a great deal of ignorance of reality. People "who have not seen a star pitched" think they know better than seasoned, experienced stargazers. At least that's what my grandmother used to say. She was right. Sadly, the realization that dad or mom knows best sometimes comes too late.

[handwritten marginal note: The reality is that God knows best what we need, for we are His created]

This attitude also indicates a lack of maturity. It often springs from a premature striving for total independence when we do not yet have wings to fly. Adam and Eve haven't been on planet Earth very long, yet they think they know more than their Maker. They think they know enough to refuse to listen to God and to follow their own instincts.

Von Rad suggests another reason why Adam and Eve ignored God, noting that the serpent implied the ". . . possibility of an extension of human existence beyond the limits set for it by God at creation, an increase of life not only in the sense of pure intellectual enrichment but also of familiarity with, and power over, mysteries that lie beyond man."[7]

That is, Adam and Eve desired to move beyond their God-ordained boundaries. God had set boundaries in all

[handwritten note at bottom: to transcend, become more than God]

of creation. He set boundaries between sea and land, heaven and the skies, animals and humans and between humans and God. In a real sense, it's this creation of boundaries that brings order out of chaos. Adam and Eve wanted to remove the ultimate boundary. They wanted to become like God.

The obliteration of sound boundaries often signals the beginning of unhealthful shame. Ray Anderson in his *Self-Care* sees a vital link between good shame and boundaries. For him, the capacity to feel shame is "part of the self's maintenance of a healthy sense of limitation and even the core of humility."[8] For Anderson, "It is our capacity for shame that enables us to live comfortably within the boundaries and limits set for us by our capabilities, our relationship with others, and our own sense of dignity and self-worth."[9] Enticed by the serpent, Adam and Eve's desire to move beyond their God-ordained boundaries indicated that they were moving toward toxic shame.

Whenever we violate any of God's boundaries, we invariably experience negative consequences. For example, God sets boundaries within marital relationships—one man, one woman brought together in a vow of fidelity to each other. When one or both break that boundary through infidelity, tremendous damage is done to the relationship. Sometimes another consequence is shame that estranges those partners.

Another example of boundary breaking may suffice. In a way it connects well to Adam and Eve's desire to be and live like God. Many of us are familiar with people who try to live like God. They try to live like super persons, acting as though they have no limits in time or energy. They usually pay a price for living that way, such as depression and burnout. But it does not end with personal consequences; it often brings heavy burdens for everyone within that person's sphere of influence.

Understanding Shame

Shame has received extensive attention in today's mental health literature. Popular authors like John Bradshaw have made it a kind of buzzword. The emphasis in these works is on the inner psychological state of mind. In contrast, biblical shame mostly emphasizes the sense of public disgrace.[10] This sense of disgrace normally springs from some personal failure.

I see little reason to maintain an artificial distinction between the inner psychological dimensions of shame and the outward, more public demonstrations. All shame seems to possess both inward and outward dimensions. This is true even when public disgrace never happens. In fact, the intensity of inward psychological pain may arise partly from a constant fear of public disgrace. In this sense, the inward shame represents an internalization of an external event that hasn't happened but is dreaded. These dynamics contribute to the painfulness and insidious nature of inward, psychological pain, which is often more severe.

Nathaniel Hawthorne's *The Scarlet Letter* makes this clear. The unfaithful wife, Hester Prynne, wears the scarlet letter A denoting her adultery. Her shame was primarily public, though she doubtless also experienced inward shame. Nevertheless, she seemed to fare much better than Arthur Dimmesdale. Pastor Dimmesdale's shame was primarily inward since it remained secret. But his shame has much more dire consequences than Hester's. At one point he told her: "Happy are you, Hester, that wear the scarlet letter openly upon your bosom! Mine burns in secret. Thou little knowest what a relief it is, after the torment of a seven years' cheat, to look into an eye that recognizes me for what I am!"[11] He found it difficult to cope with his secret shame, which became his perennial torture and contributed heavily to his ultimate demise.

Even though Bible focuses mainly on the outward physical state, this does not rule out the presence of inward dynamics. Often, outward behavior is spurred by internal mechanisms whether those are cognitive, psychological or spiritual. Both dimensions are present in the Genesis account. Adam and Eve take pains to hide their exposed selves. Behind their actions to conceal, one can surmise that there was painful inward emotion. Ray Anderson relates their nakedness to their self-perception rather than their physical exposure.[12] In other words, the nakedness they try to hide is not physical alone. Rather, they wished to conceal their perceived sense of a perverted self.

Gerhard Von Rad agrees. Commenting on the Fall narrative, he writes: "They do not react to the innocence with a spiritual consciousness of guilt; rather they are afraid of their nakedness. For the first time, in their shame they detect something like a rift that can be traced to the depths of their being."[13] This observation certainly suggests internal dimensions to their shame. A deeply unsettling disruption had taken place within the woman and the man.

What are the ramifications of the shame that Adam and Eve experienced? We find some answers in the context. First, shame alienates people from each other. It moves us away from others and strains relationships formerly bound with strong cords of affection. It can make us strangers to ourselves and to others. In the Genesis narrative, Adam and Eve's desire to hide their shame and prevent exposure of embarrassing aspects of themselves drove a wedge between the couple. Fear also became a partner in crime with shame and estranged both of them from God.

Closely related to the idea of estrangement, shame appears to be a concealing emotion. It involves the desire to hide. Shame has the following root meanings: to uncover, to expose and to wound. More than anything else, the shamed persons fears "exposure of particularly sensitive, intimate, vulnerable aspects of the self."[14] Shamed persons not only fear being stripped and left vulnerable before others, but they especially dread being exposed in their own eyes. Given that fear, shame seeks to hide the vulnerabilities of the self. This concealment seems to be both physical and psychological. Thus Adam and Eve seek to hide their internal sense of shame by hiding their nakedness from the self and each other. As noted in Chapter 7, which discusses excuses, their sense of shame also made them attempt to cover up their deed through verbal means—excuses.

Bernard Mandeville, the sixteenth-century author, captured this aspect of shame poignantly when he wrote:

> Ashamed of the many frailties they feel within, all men endeavour to hide themselves, their ugly nakedness, from each other, and wrapping up the true motives of their hearts in the specious cloak of sociableness, and their concern for the public good, they are in hopes of concealing their filthy appetites and the deformity of their desires.[15]

Our modern understanding of shame shares these beliefs. For example, Ray Anderson notes: "Shame thrives on secrecy, and secrecy is its most powerful defense. What shame fears most of all is the uncovering of the self in its wretched and disgusting condition."[16] Also, Michael Lewis emphasized that the desire to hide or disappear is an essential feature of shame.[17]

We don't have to go very far to find modern examples of this phenomenon. Cover-up has become a word almost synonymous with modern political life. We saw it in the

Watergate scandal and more recently in "Monicagate" that rocked the Clinton White House. From the apparent efforts to detract, to hide, to deflect responsibility, to blatant mendacity, one surmises that shame played a major part in both political scandals.

Shame also serves as an avoiding emotion. Because of the intense inward feelings, one usually seeks to avoid responsibility in some way. One may avoid responsibility through excuses and attempts to deflect culpability onto someone else; or it may be done through attempts to cover up one's shameful deeds; or it may be accomplished through outright denial and rationalization. We see these elements in the Genesis story.

Shame is also nonconstructive. It doesn't take the initiative in repairing damage done. In the Genesis narrative, Adam and Eve do not take any positive actions to rectify the estrangement between them. Neither do they take actions to repair their relationship with God. Instead what we see is lying, stonewalling and other efforts to pull the wool over God's eyes (as though that were possible). They succeed only in deceiving themselves. What we see here is true of shame overall. It drives us to nonconstructive actions such as blaming, excusing and hiding.

Michael Lewis refers to this nonconstructive aspect of shame as paralysis. According to him, when one has violated a standard, shame calls the violator to stop. However, it goes further. It also makes a judgment on the individual. Shame's message is: "Stop. You are no good." It is this judgment upon the self that freezes the individual into inactivity. Shame is not about making amends for wrong behavior. In fact, it is not about behavior at all. Rather, it is about a morbid preoccupation with the self that goes to any length to protect the self. However, since the self is considered bad and worthless, the individual shuts down and does not make the changes necessary to

Shame only cares about self-preservation

move in a positive direction.[18] C. S. Lewis very likely had this aspect of shame in mind when he noted: "I sometimes think that shame, mere awkward, senseless shame, does as much towards preventing good acts and straightforward happiness as any of our vices can do."[19]

In fact, shame may do more than just prevent good acts. While stymieing positive action, it may generate behaviors consistent with the negative view of the self. I have known individuals who believed that they were defective, that they were rotten to the core, who lived out their hypotheses about themselves. They confirmed their badness by indulging in wrong behaviors consistent with their defective view of themselves, as though they sought to "live down to their image."

According to Ray Anderson, shame may stimulate another kind of paralysis: It cuts off the possibility of seeking and receiving forgiveness.[20] Shame may lead to such heightened feelings of self-condemnation that shame-prone persons may find it impossible to forgive themselves. They often find it difficult to accept forgiveness from others, even God. I wonder whether shame like this caused Judas to hang himself rather than seek forgiveness from God. Shame must execute the self rather than seek the possibility of meaningful, reparative action.

shame won't allow forgiveness

One can readily see this morbid preoccupation with the self in the Genesis account. Perhaps it is this preoccupation that makes it impossible for Adam and Eve to see their contribution to the Fall. Instead they are overwhelmed with self-concerns. Each primarily seeks to protect his or her own person from blame. This self-preoccupation most likely contributes to the estrangement I noted earlier. One cannot be morbidly preoccupied with oneself and still be able to reach out to others in reconciliation.

shame this away the big picture in order to both only at self preservation

shame hinders reconciliation

Ultimately shame is a self-destructive emotion. "Shame is never helpful; it does not lead to healing, growth or reparations. It tends either to cause depression or to spur perfectionistic efforts to make up for one's deficiencies."[21] Ray Anderson even suggests that shame is not an emotion at all. Rather, he considers shame as self-abuse in which emotions are used as instruments of self-flagellation.[22] Though I believe that shame is an emotion, I agree with Anderson that it kindles self-abuse. That's why I suggest that shame is self-destructive.

Much of the time shame works its destructiveness passively. Because of the failure to take constructive action, shame slowly erodes the self from the inside out. Hawthorne's *The Scarlet Letter*, mentioned earlier, is a story that vividly describes how shame destroys persons from the inside out.

In Arthur Dimmesdale we catch a glimpse of the insidious nature of shame. Dimmesdale, the pastor, had committed adultery with Hester Prynne. Hester's sin is readily apparent since she had borne a child in her husband's absence. She publicly wore the scarlet letter A as a symbol of her shame. However, Hester protected Dimmesdale and refused to reveal the identity of her lover. Thus, Dimmesdale's sin remains secret, but it crodes both his mind and spirit. At one point in the story Hester asks Dimmesdale if he had found any peace after seven years: "'None!—nothing but despair!' he answered. 'What else could I look for, being what I am, and leading such a life as mine.'"[23] His answer is revealing. Shame, like a merciless judge, continually directed his gaze to the wretched creature he perceived himself to be. When Hester reminded him of the reverence in which he was held and the good he had done, shame would have none of it. Dimmesdale replied:

> "As concerns the good which I may appear to do, I have
> no faith in it. It must needs be a delusion. What can a
> ruined soul, like mine, effect towards the redemption

of other souls?—or a polluted soul, towards their puri-
fication? And as for the people's reverence, would it were
turned to scorn and hatred. . . . I have laughed, in bit-
terness and agony of heart, at the contrast between what
I seem and what I am! And Satan laughs at it!"[24]

Rev. Dimmesdale's reply drips with scorn and self-dis-
dain. That's the sound of shame's poison insidiously cours-
ing its way through his life until all is polluted. His desire
for the people's scorn and hatred mirrored the feelings he
held toward himself deep within. In the end, Rev. Dimmesdale comes clean publicly. He bares his chest revealing the
letter A mysteriously emblazoned in his flesh. Then he falls
and shortly dies. Secret shame had taken its toll upon him
spiritually, psychologically and physically.

Sometimes, shame may become more actively destructive. This destructive nature of shame seems to be
at work in Tolstoy's *Anna Karenina*. In that tragic tale,
Anna Karenina, a married woman, falls in love with and
later becomes sexually involved with Count Vronsky. But
Anna is never totally comfortable with her choices and
behaviors. Finally conquered by her deep shame, Anna
comes apart and commits suicide by standing in front of
an oncoming train. French author Gustave Flaubert
strikes a similar theme in his *Madame Bovary*. Overcome
with shame from repeated infidelity with disastrous consequences for her family, Madame Bovary also commits
suicide. Shame is a fire that one cannot take in one's bosom without being seriously burned.

Naming Shame

Modern authors have different names for this destructive kind of shame. For example, John Bradshaw labels
it toxic shame and distinguishes it from healthful shame.
Like Anderson, he believes that healthful shame keeps

us within the boundaries of our humanity and serves a foundation for humility and spirituality. In contrast, toxic shame weakens us and fosters a deep sense of defectiveness.[25] Other names for this unhealthful shame include narcissistic shame and disgrace shame. Whatever the name, this kind of shame is always destructive. One author described it as: ". . . fearful of exposure out of concern for the image of the self which others may develop should other people see the 'real' me with all my disgusting ways, deficiencies, and defects."[26]

This shame obviously characterized Adam and Eve. They hid from God and from themselves. They sought to cover up not only themselves but also their actions through irresponsibility, deflection of blame and denial. What possible hope could there be for persons caught in this condition? How does one get out from under the debilitating weight of toxic shame?

Michael Lewis admits that coping with shame is difficult. He suggests that owning shame is the simplest method. By owning and removing oneself from the shaming situation, shame dissipates over time. Lewis further suggests that denial, forgetting, laughter and confession may also be useful.[27] Two things strike me about these solutions. First, even when one owns his or her shame, it's not always possible to remove oneself from the shaming situation. For example, Hester Prynne's shame was owned, but she continued to wear the scarlet letter in the community. And even when one is able outwardly to remove oneself from the shaming situation, one might yet carry an internal representation of the shame. Second, denial, forgetting and laughter largely are applied to situations such as having an article rejected by a journal. These may indeed be shaming experiences, but they are not like the situations in which one has violated a critical standard. Significantly,

Lewis mentions confession and its proved effectiveness in combating shame across the centuries.

Adam and Eve evidently tried a couple of these strategies. They endeavored to escape from the situation by avoiding God, but they were not successful. They also tried denial, but that did not work. They needed more than only themselves to get beyond their shame. One thing seems evident from the Genesis account: Redemption does not readily come from within shame-prone individuals. They are too self-consumed, too paralyzed to initiate constructive, reparative, redemptive actions on their own behalf. They are far more bent on cover-up, secrecy and hiding than on the uncovering and confession that lead to healing.

The answer largely lies outside them. Someone must help save the self from the self. Individuals caught in the web of toxic shame need help from outside themselves. Rarely can these individuals rescue themselves. Such efforts often become futile exercises in frustration. Without help, the personal outcome is usually disastrous. As we have seen, sometimes the outcome of shame is spiritual or psychological suicide. We may not physically abuse ourselves for our shameful deeds, but we often psychologically whip ourselves.

So where do we get help? Genesis gives us the perfect example. Adam and Eve are redeemed from outside of themselves. God seeks, finds, uncovers and restores these shamed persons. Because of their shame, they were driven to paralysis as far as constructive, reparative action was concerned. They needed an initiating, gracious God to redeem them.

Sometimes God does this work on his own, as in the Genesis account. He certainly can go solo. However, much of the time God chooses to work in tandem with humanity. I suspect that David was engulfed in shame after his sin with Bathsheba. His efforts to cover up his actions with murder and various subterfuges fit shame's pattern. God sent Nathan to move David to guilt and confession that put him back on track. However, the ultimate example is found in the Incarnation. In this event, God sent his Son, clothed in human flesh, to redeem paralyzed humanity. He's still doing the same today—unfreezing shamed persons through the direct actions of his Spirit. But he is also working through others, through Christian healers of all sorts. And sometimes, he even uses secular healers. In varied ways, people are unfrozen and redeemed and God is glorified.

Endnotes

1. Michael Lewis, *Shame: The Exposed Self* (New York: The Free Press, 1992).

2. See Dietrich Bonhoeffer, Creation and Fall: A Theological Exposition of Genesis 1–3, D. S. Bax, trans. (Minneapolis: Fortress Press, 1997). Bonhoeffer makes this link between shame and sexuality.

3. Leo Tolstoy, *Anna Karenina* (New York: Random House, 1965), Modern Library edition, p. 95.

4. Adam Clarke, *Commentary on Genesis* (Albany, Ore.: Ages Software, Version 2.0, 1996, 1997).

5. Lewis, op. cit.

6. Gerhard Von Rad, *Genesis* (Philadelphia: Westminster Press, 1972), p. 88.

7. Ibid., p. 89.

8. Ray Anderson, *Self Care* (Wheaton Ill.: Victor Books, 1995), p. 146.

9. Ibid, p. 148.

10. See the discussion of Hebrew *bosh* in R. Laird Harrris, Gleason L. Archer, and Bruce K. Waltke, *Theological Wordbook of the Old Testament* (Chicago: Moody Press, 1980), pp. 97–98.

11. Hawthorne, Nathaniel, *The Scarlet Letter* (New York: Alfred Knopf, 1992). First published in 1850.

12. Anderson, op. cit.

13. Von Rad, op. cit., p. 91.

14. Lynd, Helen, M. *On Shame and the Search for Identity*, NY: Harcourt, Brace and Company, 1958, p. 27.

15. Bernard Mandeville, *The Fable of the Bees* (1723).

16. Anderson, op. cit., p. 158.

17. Michael Lewis, op. cit.

18. Ibid.

19. C. S. Lewis, *A Grief Observed* (New York: Seabury Press, 1963), p. 9.

20. Anderson, op. cit.

21. John M. Berecz and Herbert W. Helm, Jr., "Shame: The Underside of Christianity," in *Journal of Psychology and Christianity*, 17(1998): 1, 5–14.

22. Anderson, op. cit.

23. Hawthorne, op. cit., p. 198.

24. Ibid.

25. John Bradshaw, "Healing the Shame that Binds You" (audiocassette), (Florida: Health Communications, 1989).

26. R. H. Albers, *Shame: A Faith Perspective* (New York: Haworth Pastoral Press, 1995), p. 14.

27. Michael Lewis, op. cit., pp. 127ff.

Questions for Further Study

1. Brainstorm to create a list of positive emotions. Next, make a list of negative emotions. Circle those that could be "spiritual barometers" in our lives.

2. Why did God create us to have emotions?

3. Does secular society think that Christians consider sex a "good thing"? Why does society so often confuse God's prohibitions on sex outside of marriage with a total prohibition of sex?

4. Make a list of "other voices" clamoring for Christians' attention in your world. Which voices scream the loudest?

5. Give examples of ways we, like Adam and Eve, think we know better than God what is best for us.

6. What are some of the God-ordained boundaries in creation that humans strive to exceed?

7. Do you agree that inward, nonpublic shame can be more painful than public disgrace? Explain.

8. Do persons in our contemporary, anything-goes society still feel shame or have we lost that ability? Give examples to support your response.
9. Summarize the various ways the author says shame is self-destructive. How can shame keep us estranged from God?
10. Do you agree with the author that God often uses other human beings to "unfreeze" us from the paralysis of toxic shame and restore us to a right relationship with himself and others? Why or why not?

Chapter Nine

Guilt and Responsibility

The Absence of Guilt

There's a noticeable absence of guilt in Adam and Eve. Given their disobedience to God, guilt appears to be the most appropriate response. But guilt is strangely absent from the narrative. Gerhard Von Rad highlights this absent emotion in his commentary on this passage. Instead of guilt, fear of nakedness took center stage.[1] They demonstrated shame instead of guilt. Why is this? *shame instead of guilt*

Some would probably say that guilt is in the passage. Many people consider guilt as synonymous with shame. The confusion is understandable because both emotions involve the violation of standards. According to Michael Lewis both of these self-conscious emotions function to interrupt any action that violates one's standards.[2] Some additional features shared by shame and guilt include:

1. Both are moral emotions occurring in situations involving moral failure.

2. Both are "self-conscious" emotions.
3. Both are focused on negative aspects of either the self or behavior.
4. Both involve internal attributions of one sort or another.
5. Both are typically experienced in interpersonal contexts.[3]

However, shame and guilt differ in fundamental ways. For instance, the emotional consequences differ greatly. Shame is generally more painful than guilt. It diminishes the self in that the shamed individual feels small, worthless and powerless. In many ways, shame is a disintegrative type of experience. In contrast, the guilty person feels remorse and regret without necessarily diminishing the self. Guilt permits the integrity of the self.[4] We'll explore additional critical differences in the following sections.

[margin notes: Shame then self↓to guilt / Guilt permits integrity of self to be what]

Shame Focuses on the Self, Guilt on the Behavior

We have already seen that shame morbidly focuses on the self rather than the faulty behavior. Shame overwhelms the individual with a sense of failure that defies redemption. In the process, the self is diminished and devalued. This is one way in which shame demonstrates its destructive quality. Shame also seeks to punish its victim mercilessly.

[margin notes: shame is self focused / guilt is behavior focused]

Like shame, appropriate guilt results when one has violated a known standard of behavior. However, unlike shame, guilt focuses on the wrong deed done instead of on the person. Guilt focuses upon behavior because its purpose is redemptive; it seeks to get the individual back on the right track by influencing him or her to repair the wrong done. In *Uncovering Shame*, Harper and Hoopes had this to say about guilt:

[margin notes: A the deed was irresponsible, but you are not a bad person; guilt / shame says you are a bad person]

[bottom handwritten note: guilt & redemption, God created us to feel guilt to help the restoration process]

[handwritten: guilt an evaluation of behavior]

... [G]uilt is an evaluation of *behavior*. When people recognize that their behavior has violated some standard that has meaning to them, they feel guilty for having done it. Guilt is emotionally healthy and a necessary process of living with others, as long as it is an evaluation of behavior rather than being, leads to changing of behavior, and is not chronically excessive.[5]

[handwritten: shame a negative evaluation of being]

Unlike shame, guilt can be removed. We unburden ourselves in two ways. We can fulfill the consequences of our behavior that have been meted out, or we can confess our wrongs and receive pardon and forgiveness. Either way permits the offender to wipe the slate clean.[6]

Michael Lewis has noted that shame calls the individual to stop. But shame does more. It makes a statement about the person's worth. Guilt is different. It, too, says "Stop!" but it calls attention to the behavior and the violated standard. Its goals are to alert, to provoke anxiety about wrong behavior and to correct the inappropriate behavior.[7] In contrast, shame pronounces the badness of the self and then takes pains to cover up the shameful deed.

[handwritten: alert, provoke and correct]

[handwritten: shame seeks to cover up]

Sometimes an individual may experience feelings of both shame and guilt. In such cases the removal of guilt may do nothing to remove the feelings of shame. Ray Anderson suggests that we may be experiencing shame instead of guilt when we have legitimately sought forgiveness but have not sensed any release from culpability.[8] Other authors suggest that guilt experiences only become maladaptive when they become fused with shame.[9]

Shame Detracts from Responsibility, Guilt Takes Responsibility

A second major difference between shame and guilt involves the issue of responsibility. Because of the morbid preoccupation with the self, shame pays little, if any,

Shame deflects responsibility in order to cover up perceived badness, guilt invites responsibility

attention to transgressions or redressing them.[10] In my opinion, this self-orientation in shame stymmies responsibility and prevents correction of misdeeds. It's too consumed with covering perceived badness to care about responsibility. In fact, shame deflects responsibility through excuses or blaming others, as we see in the Genesis account of the Fall. In contrast, guilt invites contriteness and accepting responsibility.[11] The Genesis account of the Fall offers little evidence for anything resembling guilt.

Shame Covers, Guilt Uncovers

Shame hides, keep secret

In the chapter on shame I mentioned the metaphor of covering as integral to shame. That is, shame usually seeks to hide its deeds. It always leads to concealment out of fear of doing further damage to the self. Shame revolves around secrecy. This secretive aspect of shame suggests that it may possess some addictive features. I have found that in almost all addictions, secrecy is a major component and the very life-blood of the addiction.

Shame's addiction is self preservation

Shame's addiction is the protection of the exposed self at all costs. Because of shame's fear of exposure, it may have short-circuited the guilt response in Adam and Eve. After all, one cannot hide one's offense (shame's response) and still expose and confess it at the same time (guilt's response).

Considering this notion of covering, shame seems the dominant emotion in David's sin with Bathsheba (2 Samuel 11). David had committed adultery with Bathsheba, Uriah's wife. When David discovered she was pregnant, he tried to cover up his sin by sending Uriah home from the front to sleep with his wife, hoping Uriah would think that he was in fact the father of Bathsheba's child. When this ploy failed, David secretly had Uriah murdered. The efforts to conceal the sin, the disruption

Does guilt lead to shame? If left by itself?

of relationships, the deflection of responsibility from himself and the prominence of secrecy all suggest shame's presence. *and self preservation*

The opposite is true of guilt. Rather than seeking to cover, guilt uncovers one's actions and makes appropriate reparations. It seeks to make amends. Again, in David we find a good biblical example of this process of uncovering and coming clean before God. For example, in Psalm 32 David wrote: *guilt an uncomfortableness??*

guilt uncovers

> Blessed is he whose transgression is forgiven, whose sin is covered. Blessed is the man to whom the LORD imputes no iniquity, and in whose spirit there is no deceit. When I declared not my sin, my body wasted away through my groaning all day long. For day and night thy hand was heavy upon me; my strength was dried up as by the heat of summer. I acknowledged my sin to thee, and I did not hide my iniquity; I said, "I will confess my transgressions to the LORD "; then thou didst forgive the guilt of my sin (Psalm 32:1–5).

The passage reveals that there was a time that instead of uncovering his sin, David hid his sin. That strategy brought nothing but trouble. He experienced wasting of his body and constant emotional turmoil. When he finally came clean and confessed his sin, he experienced forgiveness and relief from turmoil.

Psalm 32:1 is a telling verse. David refers to forgiveness and having one's sin covered as a happy state. This suggests that covering is not a bad thing in itself. In fact, covering is necessary. The problem is that we often seek to cover ourselves. What we really need is God's covering. Our covering does not address our sin and need for atonement, but instead pretends that no violation has occurred. Alas, it is woefully lacking. We remain buried in our sin and shame. The Genesis account testifies to this reality. Adam and Eve's patchwork attempt at cover-

we need God's covering, which is forgiveness

our covering is much too little, for we are God's created

ing didn't get the job done. God himself had to provide adequate covering for their nakedness. That nakedness involved their whole being: their physical bodies, their emotional turmoil and their spiritual need.

The Guilting Process

Many of the features of guilt we have noted are part of what has been called the guilting process, which has six steps:

1. Recognition of wrongdoing
2. Knowledge of penalties and rewards
3. Feelings of remorse and sorrow
4. Recognition of strain on relationships
5. Expectations for repair
6. Having choices and consequences[12]

Responsibility, regret, resolve, repair

These steps need little explanation, with the exception of steps 5 and 6. "Expectations for repair" means that the violator knows the behaviors that are necessary to make things right. "Having choices and consequences" means that the guilty person has some choice about what actions to take but knows that consequences will remain.

All must know and must do them

Laura Schlessinger, the popular syndicated columnist and radio personality, speaks of the four R's of repentance: responsibility, regret, resolve and repair. One must recognize wrongs and take responsibility, demonstrate remorse for actions and the pain caused and resolve never to repeat the actions regardless of circumstances. Finally, one must actively take steps to repair any damage done and apologize to the injured party. When these steps are taken, forgiveness should result.

Psalms 51 reveals many aspects of this guilting process. David wrote the psalm after Nathan the prophet had

4 R's of repentance.

responsibility, regret, resolve, repair.

confronted him regarding his sin with Bathsheba. Evidently God's strategy had worked. Prior to this confrontation, David had used shaming behaviors in which he sought to hide his deed. He had even shown "righteous indignation" at Nathan's story of a rich man who had robbed a poor man of his one lamb (2 Samuel 12).

To the psychologically astute, David's anger at the injustice is an excellent example of reaction formation. In this defense mechanism, persons speak out against behaviors in which they themselves participate. Following David's fierce judgment, Nathan drove home his piercing dart: "Thou are the man!" David was shocked from his shame into a more appropriate emotion, guilt. David immediately responded with confession: "I have sinned against the LORD" (2 Samuel 12:13).

I do not mean to impose the guilting process on this psalm artificially. However, many of the features naturally fit the passage. We'll look at a few examples; you may find others. David recognizes his wrongdoing in the memorable opening verses:

Have mercy on me, O God, according to thy steadfast love; according to thy abundant mercy blot out my transgressions. Wash me thoroughly from my iniquity, and cleanse me from my sin! For I know my transgressions, and my sin is ever before me. Against thee, thee only, have I sinned, and done that which is evil in thy sight, so that thou art justified in thy sentence and blameless in thy judgment (Psalm 51:1–4).

David obviously knew the penalty attached to sinful behavior. He also knew the rewards of righteousness. The former included God's sentence and judgment (v. 4) and the loss of God's presence and Holy Spirit (v. 12). Likewise he knew that righteous obedience meant joy and gladness (v. 8), a clean heart and a right spirit (v. 10) and restoration of salvation and God's upholding (v. 12). We do not have to search for feelings of sorrow and remorse. The entire psalm is a cry from a soul tormented with sorrow and grief. Likewise we readily see the strain David's sin had done to his relationship with God as David lost the sense of God's presence. David also knew what he needed to do to rectify his sin and repair his relationship with God. It's embodied in one word, confession. And that's what this psalm is all about. David chose to acknowledge his sin and seek forgiveness. However, many consequences would yet remain. David lost the child that had resulted from his sin. For many years afterwards, his whole family would experience the reverberations of his sin. Sins and bloodshed would cling to his family.

A similar guilting response is what one would have expected to see in Adam and Eve, but it is regrettably absent. Rather we see a shame response characterized by efforts to cover up. I wonder if God's questioning of the couple was designed to do what Nathan's story did for David—to bring them to owning culpability for their sin. That's what they needed to do to get back on track.

Healthful Guilt

When persons experience this guilting process as David did, they are experiencing healthful guilt. "Healthy guilt is the recognition people have when they have failed to meet the expectations of someone with whom they have a significant relationship and to whom they feel accountable."[13] Healthy guilt opens the door to recovery and redemption. In this sense, guilt is a worthy emotion. It is the appropriate and healthy response to wrongdoing when related to hurt inflicted on others. It is not always psychologically destructive as some would suggest. In fact research demonstrates that appropriate guilt is unrelated to maladjustment except when wedded to shame.[14]

To speak of healthful guilt flies in the face of conventional wisdom. Many people castigate those who use the language of guilt, believing that fostering guilt is always wrong and inappropriate. They vehemently argue against guilt being psychologically healthful. For example, noted therapists such as Albert Ellis consider guilt and seeking to observe standards of right and wrong as the basis for neuroses, not health. I disagree. Where there is legitimate wrong, guilt is the appropriate response. More than that, guilt is the *healthful* response.

When individuals have violated standards, they need to be held responsible for their actions. To do otherwise is to mistake enabling behavior for true love. True love always seeks the good of the one who is loved. Sometimes love will demand that one be confronted with his or her wrong actions. However, the emphasis will be upon the reparative actions needed, not on disparaging the character of the person.

False Guilt

Of course, there is an unhealthful guilt. I have often encountered persons who struggle with this debilitating kind of guilt. Usually there is little basis for the "guilt" that they felt. Rather, these persons seem to be plagued by "fantasized transgressions." For instance, in an earlier chapter, I presented the example of Kathy who was always bailing out her irresponsible adult sister Kim. Whenever Kathy stopped supporting Kim's irresponsibility, she felt a false guilt whose pangs were just as real as true guilt.

Or let's consider Sherry. Sherry was almost fifty years old, although she looked much older. One of her problems was "guilt" about her brother who had died. Every week Sherry had faithfully visited her brother who was in a nursing home. During one period of time, Sherry

Created for Responsiblity

herself became ill and was unable to visit her brother.
Unfortunately, during her illness, her brother died. Sherry
was racked with fictional guilt. Although she was unable
to be with him at the time of his death, she felt she had
not been there for her brother, and her feelings of guilt
were very real to her.

An extreme form of guilt from fantasized transgressions is sometimes seen in those persons who believe they
have committed the unpardonable sin. In many cases,
these are persons who love God deeply. However, they
have become morbidly focused on every infirmity, every
slip of human frailty, as a sign of grievous sin. Usually
there is no basis for their guilt.

Real guilt proceeds from a violation of some standard
or rule and concern for those hurt by the behavior. Real
guilt comes from real sin—from violating God's standards. Where there is no sin, there is no true guilt. Guilt
might also flow from violation of society's or our own
standards for behavior. As we saw earlier in the guilting
process, real guilt must show concern for those hurt by
the behavior. It must also seek to heal the damage done
to the person and the relationship.

Exposure to the truth and relabeling false guilt are
sometimes useful strategies for addressing unnecessary
guilt. For instance, Kathy would do well to see how her
enabling of her sister is actually harmful rather than helpful. One could then reframe financial nonsupport as the
most useful expression of love for her sister. Kathy could
also be helped to relabel what she called "guilt" as "discomfort." She had become accustomed to taking care of
her sister. Though problematic, it was a familiar response.
Not taking care of her sister was a new response that felt
uncomfortable by the very nature of its newness.

In a way her response is akin to discarding an old pair
of shoes for a new pair. The old pair feels comfortable

[margin notes:] Authentic guilt not based in reality

[margin note:] Real guilt seeks to restore

△ Don't mistake discomfort w/ guilt.

but provides no protection for the feet. By contrast, the new pair provides good protection but takes getting used to. The new shoes may feel different and perhaps a bit uncomfortable. But if one sticks with the new shoes, they, too, will begin to feel comfortable. People feeling false guilt need to know that if they persist in the appropriate behavior, it will become more comfortable.

Finding the Way Back: The Rediscovery of Guilt

When we violate standards, guilt is appropriate response. Guilt is the road back to a place of healthful emotions and repairing of relationships. But that can happen only if we acknowledge responsibility and take reparative steps. Sometimes we take steps that lead us away from acknowledging guilt. We may see guilt as an unworthy emotion and use various psychological methods to avoid dealing with it. Therapeutic methods may become a bowl of psychological pottage substituted for our spiritual birthright. Perpetual shame is one of the emotional ramifications of this approach. *this guilt, when not dealt with can lead to shame*

When I was a doctoral student, I read an article by psychologist Peter Marin entitled "Living in Moral Pain."[15] It dealt primarily with Vietnam vets, who were often treated for emotional disorders such as Post-Traumatic Stress Disorder (PTSD). But Marin was surprised to discover the world of moral pain in which some vets lived. He suggested that much of their pain and anger sprang from a profound moral distress because they realized they had committed acts with real and terrible consequences. Thus they experienced not only psychological stress but also moral pain—in other words, guilt.

For Marin guilt is not simply a psychological phenomenon. Rather it is a moral emotion that has definite psychological value. This moral dimension must be taken seriously. When ignored, therapists may focus exclusively on psychological phenomena such as PTSD and miss components of guilt present in some of their patients' experiences. No amount of therapy adequately deals with moral pain. An avenue for confession must be found if those veterans were to fully recover.

Strangely enough, Marin found a tendency to ignore guilt in the literature about Vietnam veterans. In his words ". . . various phrases are used to empty the vets' experience of moral content, to diffuse and bowdlerize it."[16] For instance, the effects of slaughter and atrocity were simply labeled "stress." This seems to fit our cultural pattern. As Marin observes,

> We seem as a society to have few useful ways to approach moral pain or guilt; it remains for us a form of neurosis or a pathological symptom, something to escape from rather than something to learn from, a disease rather than—as it may well be for the vets—an appropriate if painful response to the past.[17]

Marin reported that one psychologist told him that he and his colleagues never dealt with guilt. Rather, they treated the vets' difficulties as problems in adjustment. No wonder many remained in moral pain. Fortunately, Marin found some professionals who understood the reality of guilt providing counseling to veterans. One such individual reported: "We aren't just counselors; we are almost priests. They come to us for absolution as well as for help."[18]

This insight from Marin provides compelling testimony to the reality of guilt. It also reveals our society's reluctance to take guilt seriously, even though ignoring guilt locks its victims in an hopeless world of moral pain and frustration. Evidently, we need to rediscover guilt as a healthful response and embrace it as the doorway to recovery.

An Old Story Revisited

The biblical story of the Prodigal Son in Luke 15:11–32, told by Jesus himself, demonstrates the power of guilt as a path to recovery. In this familiar story, the younger brother defied convention and demanded his share of his father's estate. In the far country of sin he squandered his property in debauched living.

The basis for his downfall is same as that displayed in our foreparents, Adam and Eve. It's the same force that drives many of us to ruin—the ancient sin of disobedience. Disobedience to convention and to his father brought the wayward son to desolation. He eventually found himself competing with pigs for his daily meal. What a fall!

How does he get out of the swine pit and find a place of redemption? He followed the very same route each of us must take when we fall into sin and disobedience. If you look carefully at the story, you will find many of the aspects of the guilting process. The process begins with a return to "sanity." Gestalt therapists have a famous saying: "Lose your mind and come to your senses." The opposite is true here. He finds his mind and comes to his senses. In Luke 15:18, he says, "I will arise and go to my father, and I will say to him, 'Father, I have sinned against heaven and before you.'"

The resolve expressed in that verse suggests a couple of things about healthful guilt. First, any effective, healthful guilt must culminate in a decision regarding appropriate action(s) we need to take. Mere thoughts about guilt never heal unless they push us to reparative actions. We must arise and do something about our misdeeds.

Second, healthful guilt always begins with taking responsibility for what we have done wrong. It does not shirk responsibility or hide behind lame excuses. It does not say, "Yes, but . . ." It accepts responsibility.

If you look closely at the passage you will find the other aspects of the guilt process. This rebellious younger son evidently knows about penalties. He knows he is not worthy to be called a son any longer. He is resigned to being a hired servant. As in David's case, remorse and sorrow are hallmarks of the story. There's also evidence to support his recognition of strain in the relationship with his father. This fallen son's behavior had driven a wedge between his father and his brother and between him and his brother. All relationships connected to him had suffered grievously. It's also clear that he knew confession was the appropriate action if he wished to attempt to repair the damaged relationships. The younger son made the right choice when he decided to confess.

Then there's the matter of consequences. They are all over the story and they are spiritual, psychological and physical. He cannot change his experience. The memories of fair-weather friends, want of bread and groveling in a pig's sty were forever seared in his memory. He could wipe out his guilt through confession and forgiveness, but he could not erase the memories of his harsh journey into sin and disobedience. Those would remain as constant reminders, the stigmata of his sin. Finally, he had lost all of his earthly resources.

One detail seems to differ from the guilt process, which has to do with his knowledge of rewards. He seems strangely lacking in this area. He obviously did not fully anticipate the magnanimity of a loving father and the reward of full acceptance back into his father's house. He expected at most the role of a servant. He is surprised by joy in his father's graciousness:

> But the father said to his servants, "Bring quickly the best robe, and put it on him; and put a ring on his hand, and shoes on his feet; and bring the fatted calf and kill it, and let us eat and make merry; for this my son was

dead, and is alive again; he was lost, and is found." And they began to make merry (Luke 15:22–24).

What a welcome! New clothing, a ring on his finger, shoes on his feet, food in abundance, the warm presence of caring people, joy and merriment! Totally unexpected! The prodigal son had found his way back home. But his road to recovery came through taking responsibility, confession and a healthy dose of guilt.

Endnotes

1. Gerhard Von Rad, *Genesis* (Philadelphia: Westminster Press, 1972), p. 91.

2. Michael Lewis, *Shame: The Exposed Self* (New York: The Free Press, 1992).

3. June P. Tangney, "Shame and Guilt in Interpersonal Relationships," in *Self-Conscious Emotions,* eds. June P. Tangney and Kurt W. Fischer (New York: Guilford Press, 1995), p. 116.

4. Ibid.

5. James M. Harper and Margaret H. Hoopes, *Uncovering Shame: Integrating Individuals and Their Family Systems* (New York: Norton, 1990), p. 3.

6. Ray Anderson, *Self Care* (Wheaton Ill.: Victor Books, 1995), p. 151.

7. Lewis, op. cit.

8. Anderson, op. cit.

9. June P. Tangney, Susan A. Burggraf, and Patricia E. Wagner, "Shame-Proneness, Guilt-Proneness and Psychological Symptoms," in *Self-Conscious Emotions,* eds. June P. Tangney and Kurt W. Fischer (New York: Guilford Press, 1995).

10. M. Fossom and M. Mason, *Facing Shame: Families in Recovery* (New York: W. W. Norton, 1986).

11. Ibid.

12. Harper and Hoopes, op. cit., pp. 62–63.

13. Ibid., p. 61–62.

14. Tangney, Burggraf, and Wagner, op. cit.

15. Peter Marin, "Living in Moral Pain," *Psychology Today,* November 1981, pp. 68–80.

16. Ibid., p. 72.

17. Ibid., p. 71

18. Ibid., p. 68.

Questions for Further Study

1. Before reading this book, did you consider guilt as synonymous with shame? Do you now agree with the author that they are separate emotions? Why or why not?

2. Give examples from your life of concrete ways guilt has spurred you to change a sinful behavior or repair a wrong you have committed. How did you feel after these experiences with guilt?

3. When you feel upset after you've done something wrong, how can you tell whether you are feeling shame, guilt or a mixture of both?

4. What are the top three methods (based on your observations of human nature) that people who feel shame use to cover up things they have done wrong?

5. Do you agree with the author that guilt can be healthful, or do you side with those who consider guilt a destructive emotion? Explain your reasoning.

6. What is the difference between enabling someone in his or her wrongdoing versus confronting that person's sin in a loving way? Why does the enabling behavior often feel to us like love?

7. Why did the therapists who were observed by Peter Marin while treating Vietnam veterans avoid exploring the moral dimension of their patients' suffering?

8. Why doesn't our society take guilt more seriously, choosing instead to ignore guilt, thus locking its victims in endless moral pain and frustration?

Chapter Ten

Grace and Responsibility

Unseen Grace

How easily we disregard grace amidst the turmoil and chaos following the Fall! Sin and shame, fear and failure deeply punctuate the narrative. Caught beneath this tragic, foreboding shadow, we can be blinded to the delicate footprints of grace. Masaccio missed it in his famous painting, *Expulsion from Paradise*. He captured the grim scene in all its poignancy—the pain, the disgrace, the torment of human souls in terrible agony—but he missed grace. He depicted Adam and Eve clothed with leaves as they are driven forth from Paradise. He envisioned them cast forth into a harsh, new world without adequate protection and provision. I suspect he was taking artistic license to highlight the lowest point of human history. Whatever the reason, the painting obscures the presence of grace.

This omission may partly spring from the character of grace. Grace does not loudly announce itself. Grace

Grace is The basis, all for our Good

appears like a well-bred lady who draws no attention to her arrival, even though her presence brings an air of distinction to any gathering. Although unnoticed, she exudes a sweet, transforming presence. Nevertheless, her presence is imperceptible, silent and powerful. People who are primarily attracted to the dramatic can easily miss such unpretentious grace. Grace is not so much evident in its arrival as in its transforming power. We may not notice the transformation immediately. Like yeast worked through dough, grace is most clearly seen after it has had time to work in an impoverished life.

Once we learn the rules for discerning grace, we are overwhelmed with its presence in the early chapters of Genesis. We certainly do not expect to find it amidst the tragedy of the Fall, but it's there. Grace shouts exultantly from the early scenes in Genesis. But it does not always appear with the same voice or visage. Sometimes it's in the sheer lavishness with which God prepares the world for his human guests. At other times, grace creates firm boundaries within which we enhance our lives. Grace also speaks the language of prohibition: "Thou shalt not." But it's all grace. Since it derives from God's presence, we find its many manifestations in the varied images of God. I shall say more about these images of grace later.

The Meaning of Grace

But what is this grace of which I speak? Grace has been defined as the unmerited favor of God. It's something we don't deserve. It flows freely from God's love and care for his creation. In fact, we most keenly encounter grace in the midst of outright rebellion against God. Paul's famous words distill the very heart of grace: ". . . where sin increased, grace abounded all the more" (Romans 5:20b). It shines at its best when sin is at its worst. Nowhere is this more true than in the Fall narrative. At the height of humanity's greatest sin, grace abounded all the more.

Grace that Goes Before

But grace does more than superabound where sin abounds. Grace anticipates and precedes sin. We first catch a glimpse of this grace in Genesis 3 after the Fall. It is God who initiates contact with his fallen creatures. Buried in shame and fear and with little sensibility of their sin, they hid from God. They lacked the will and the desire to seek him. He had to seek them out if they were to be redeemed. That's always the picture of grace: God initiating and seeking fallen creatures.

Theologians call this *prevenient* grace—grace that goes before human need and human sin. Grace is absolutely necessary to our response to God. Without this grace, we are absolutely incapable of responding to God. "Prevenient Grace effects a partial restoring of our sin-corrupted human faculties, sufficient that we might sense our need and God's offer of salvation, and respond to that offer."[1] This restoration includes a renewal of our understanding so that we might grasp the knowledge of divine things. It also helps our conscience to discern the difference between good and evil. Prevenient grace restores the human capacity to respond to the awareness of God.[2]

Why do we need such restoration to respond to God? It's because of the disruption of our spiritual sensitivities. Prior to the Fall, Adam and Eve were innocent and had clear vision to see and know spiritual things. Famed commentator Matthew Henry said this about Adam:

> His understanding saw Divine things clearly and truly; there were no errors or mistakes in his knowledge; his will consented at once, and in all things, to

the will of God. His affections were all regular, and
he had no bad appetites or passions. His thoughts
were easily brought and fixed to the best subjects.
Thus holy, thus happy, were our first parents in having the image of God upon them.[3]

What a difference the Fall made! Prior to the Fall,
Adam and Eve relished God's presence. They valued their
time with him and experienced sweet communion. After
their sin, they cringed and hid from God. Their spiritual
sensitivities of wrong had been deeply fractured. They
found it difficult to comprehend and own their sin. God
must work with them and spell out the true heinous nature of their sin. How are they to see their sin and respond to God? Only through the grace God provides. The
same is true for every son and daughter of Adam and Eve.
He must enable us to respond to him and to spiritual
things.

This enabling of the human capacity to respond to
God makes grace responsible. Randy Maddox, author of
Responsible Grace, writes ". . . Grace *inspires* and *enables*, but does not *overpower*."[4] He noted that this was
the sense in which John Wesley saw grace as co-operant
(another word for *responsible*). It enables us to respond
but never coerces our response.

Grace from God's Presence

Ultimately grace springs from the presence of God. Where
God is absent there is no possibility of grace. Wesley understood this. For him grace was the loving presence of
God at work in our lives: God present in the Holy Spirit
"initiating, sustaining our recovery of Christ-likeness."[5]
Wherever chaos abounds, God's presence can bring order. He can do this within all of his creation. His presence through the Spirit brought order. That's true not

only of disordered things; God's presence also brings the possibility of restoration to disordered lives. As long as God is present, there's hope.

Grace as a Call to Live Responsibly

Grace does more than enable our response to God. Grace places demands upon us to live responsibly. That's one of the first images we see of God as he relates to humans. He calls us to live responsibly. Once we have encountered grace, we cannot remain as we are. As a response to grace, we must seek to live responsibly in this world.

Responsible Christian living means many things. Earlier I indicated that it involves the choices we make regarding our thoughts, emotions, behaviors and character. Responsible living also means that we exert care in various aspects of our lives. Earlier I spoke about five areas: spiritual, social, sexual, survival and significance/service. These are fundamental to the responsible life.

Ultimately, responsible living is bound up with our relationships. Thus, we must appropriately answer to relationships on both the vertical and horizontal levels. Responding on the vertical dimension means that we are answerable to God. How will we respond to God's mandates and God's grace? H. Richard Niebuhr has described various images that capture the general character of our lives. One of these images is the image of "man-the-answerer." That's essentially who we are—responsive creatures meant to answer to God. God speaks first to us and we must answer. We are accountable to him. Whatever he says to us we must do if we will do well. We dare not ignore any word God speaks to us.[6]

We must also live responsibly on the horizontal level. This means that we must appropriately respond to ourselves, others and creation. Throughout this book, I have

responsibility to creation

not emphasized our relationship to creation to any length, choosing rather to focus on how we relate to God, self and others. However, we should never forget that living responsibly to God, self and others will also dictate how we use and care for creation.

Having said that, relating to others and self is critical. In terms of grace, answering ourselves will often mean dealing graciously with ourselves. Since God has extended grace to us, we learn to mimic this grace in dealing with ourselves. Many people who experience God's grace invalidate it by failing to respond to themselves with the same grace God showed them.

Grace also means that we must respond to others with graciousness. To fail to do so is one way we nullify God's grace in our own lives. You might remember the story of the unforgiving debtor told by Jesus in Matthew 18:23–35. One debtor owed his king millions of dollars that he could not repay. The king ordered that he, his wife, his children and all his possessions be sold to repay the debt. The desperate debtor pleaded with the king for patience. The king, filled with compassion and grace, forgave him the whole debt. Fresh from the king's magnanimous graciousness, the debtor went out and found a fellow servant who owed him a few thousand dollars. He grabbed the poor fellow by the throat and demanded instant payment. His fellow servant pleaded with the same words the other debtor had just used before the king, but to no avail. The unforgiving debtor had his colleague arrested and jailed until the debt could be repaid.

The news of the debtor's great callousness to his fellow servant was brought to the king. Understandably, the king was greatly angered. He sent for the ungracious debtor and castigated him with these words: "'You wicked servant! I forgave you all that debt because you besought me; and should not you have had mercy on your fellow servant, as I had mercy on you?' And in anger his lord delivered him to the jailers, till he should pay all his debt. So also my heavenly Father will do to every one of you, if you do not forgive your brother from your heart" (Matthew 18:32–35).

The message is clear. Grace extended to us means that we must offer grace to others. Extending grace may mean many different things in different situations. But it is clear that in this case, grace means we must forgive others. In fact, Jesus told the story in response to Peter's query about how many times one ought to forgive someone who sins against him. Jesus made it clear that it was not a matter of keeping track of the number of offenses. We forgive just as God forgives us. Grace begets grace. God extends grace to us; we extend grace to others. To do otherwise is to nullify God's grace in our own lives.

The whole notion of grace demanding responsible living may sound a bit strange to some. But that's only if we misunderstand the nature of grace or responsibility. Some people misunderstand grace as a license to do whatever one chooses. There are also misconceptions about responsibility. To some, responsibility conjures up a picture of additional loads that burden us. It's something to be avoided and disdained. One hopes that after reading the preceding chapters, that misunderstanding of responsibility has changed.

Once we understand these truths, we may see the call to responsibility as an act of grace. We begin to realize that God really favors us when he calls us to be more than we are. That's exactly what responsibility does. By responding appropriately to God, we open the door to truly becoming what God intended. Through appropriate answering to God, Adam and Eve could move from untested innocence to a place of a moral, holy character.

The Many Faces of Grace

Many other images of grace appear in Genesis. Sometimes grace comes in unexpected forms and unexpected places but it's still grace. Whatever its form or wherever it shows itself, God is there. That's because grace depends on God's presence. Therefore, we can trace its footprints by focusing on the images of God we encounter.

Grace in Creation

One of the first images that speaks of grace is creation itself. Grace silently dominates the whole story of creation. Nothing demanded that God create a world, but he chose to. In God's creative acts we see the image of a most gracious host. He prepares a world ahead of time to greet his crowning act of creation, human beings. More than that, he chose to create and fashion us in his image. That word is not spoken in relation to any other part of creation, only of humans.

God's grace is laid into the fabric of creation

David evidently was awed by God's grace in creation. He wrote:

> When I look at thy heavens, the work of thy fingers, the moon and the stars which thou hast established; what is man that thou art mindful of him, and the son of man that thou dost care for him? Yet thou hast made him little less than God, and dost crown him with glory and honor. Thou hast given him dominion over the works of thy hands; thou hast put all things under his feet, all sheep and oxen, and also the beasts of the field, the birds of the air, and the fish of the sea, whatever passes along the paths of the sea. O LORD, our Lord, how majestic is thy name in all the earth! (Psalm 8:3–9).

David evidently knew that creation was all of grace. We humans could do nothing to merit our creation. Neither did we do anything to merit our signal place in creation.

Dietrich Bonhoeffer suggested that God's creation of humans sprang from his joy of beholding in Adam the reflection of himself. Adam is a creature, but what a creature! "He is a creature, and yet he is destined to be like his Creator. Adam is 'as God.' His destiny is to bear this mystery in gratitude and obedience toward his Maker."[7] And yet in the face of such grace, the original couple still erred. They allowed the serpent to deceive them into thinking they needed to do something to become like God. Thus they sought to achieve that likeness by deciding and acting for themselves. Their choice to disobey meant a~~ ~~*about the* rejection of the grace of God. Instead of accepting grace, *Grace from* the couple chose to explore the mystery of their being by *God perceived,* themselves and apart from God.[8] *because God never left them*

Grace in Limits

We encounter another image of God in creation. God portrayed himself as one who sets limits and boundaries. Before the Spirit of God moved over the waters, all was confusion and chaos. The world was one dreadful, undifferentiated mass. God brought order out of disorder by creating boundaries. He also did so by determining the rules to govern the structures he was creating He does this by gathering some things and separating others. Read the narrative again and notice language that highlights the establishment of boundaries and limits, words such as "separation," "gathering" and "after its kind."

God doesn't only do this with created things. He also does it with created people. For example, God decided that animals are not the best kind of company for Adam. He, too, needed one after his own kind for fellowship and procreation. Thus, Eve is created as "bone of his bone and flesh of his flesh." This seems to connote that Eve is after Adam's kind. Adam and Eve must relate to and steward creation. But ultimately God placed a boundary of intimacy around the pair, one that they must not violate for any other person or thing.

God set his boundaries in another way when he set limits for Adam and Eve. They are called to avoid the tree of knowledge of good and evil. This is the very limit that the serpent invited Eve to exceed when he invited her to consider ". . . the possibility of an extension of human existence beyond the limits set for it by God at creation, an increase of life not only in the sense of pure intellectual enrichment but also of familiarity with, and power over, mysteries that lie beyond man."[9]

One ancient poet wrote: "There is a rule for all things; there are in fine fixed and stated limits, on either side of which righteousness cannot be found. On the line of duty alone we must walk."[10] Evidently, God agrees. Because he created us for righteousness, he ordained rules and limits to set us on the path to righteousness. According to Adam Clark, famed Wesleyan commentator, that's exactly what intelligent creatures need. They need rules that remind them of their dependence and accountability to God. "Man must ever feel God as his sovereign, and act under his authority, which he cannot do unless he have a rule of conduct."[11] Thus, if Adam and Eve are to enjoy God and created things, some limits must be set. There are some boundaries they must not cross. They need a rule to guide their conduct. God gave them an abundance of freedom, but it's freedom within limits.

That's always the nature of human freedom. The idea of absolute freedom is a myth. Those who try to live as though this myth were true bring disaster on themselves and society. In reality, we always live within prescribed limits set by God. As he does here with the original couple, he does with all of us. He lays out boundaries that we ought not to cross. We always cross his boundaries at a tremendous price to our well-being. The limit itself, then,

[margin handwritten note: Rules to remind us of our accountability and dependence on God]

[bottom handwritten note: responsibility is not crossing God's boundaries for us]

is a symbol of grace for it protects us from great personal pain and disaster. Limits do more than protect us; they also promote self-discovery. We learn what's a part of us and what is not. H. Richard Niebuhr reflected this reality when he noted: "We come to self-awareness if not to self-existence in the midst of *mores*, of commandments and rules, *Thou shalts* and *Thou shalt nots*, of direction and permission."[12]

Besides God, others also place limits upon us. This limit-setting starts fairly early. If we have wise parents, they begin at a very early age to sets limits for us. Later on we discover that all levels of society set limits and rules. We find limits at school, at work and in the laws of society. Each rule is intended to lay out the path to responsible living. When we follow these rules and limits, we generally do well. Slowly, over time we come to inculcate these norms as a part of our way of being. We come to realize that though we resisted them, the limits were grace in disguise.

When we violate those limits, we do not experience greater freedom as we often think we will. Rather, we experience a curtailing of freedom. Society must put in place greater limits that restrict our freedom. Those new limits come dressed in the garb of police, judges and juries. They are ultimately concretized in bars and prison walls. These become necessary to put the brakes on perceived freedom run amok.

Some might disagree with this notion of finding grace in limits, which pain them. But it's true. I often hear an ad on our local Christian station that demonstrates this. In the radio spot, a man warns a mother that her son is running in the street. The mother, offended by this intruder, begins to berate the would-be do-gooder. She accuses him of trying to inflict his own views on others. The man asks: "But, lady, don't you care about your son?"

"Of course I do!" She retorts. "That's why I wouldn't dare put limits on his freedom."

Following this exchange, one hears the dull thud of a boy being struck by a car. True grace would have set limits on where that child could play.

Sometimes we are like this fictional mom. We tend to be permissive in ways that are destructive. We sometimes take a laissez-faire attitude to discipline of our children, allowing them to virtually do anything they want. This permissive attitude springs from a misguided show of love. True love and grace set limits and boundaries. Parents ought to know and cling to this thought even when kids rebel. The child is green, ignorant and immature. He hasn't learned the ropes. He is prone to consider boundaries and responsibility as stifling. Only with maturity and the increase in wisdom does a child realize that responsibility has borne bountiful fruit. Finally, children come to realize that responsibility's stringent demands formed the catalyst for maturity and holy character. Rather than a disservice, responsibility was the means through which parents breathed grace into their children's lives.

Grace at the Bottom

One should not miss another image of grace in the Fall portion of the Genesis story. I alluded to it in the discussion of prevenient grace. Even in this dark and ominous picture, there is some good news: Sometimes hitting bottom and coming to the end of oneself creates an opportunity for God to work. Hitting bottom does not have to be the end. It can be a beginning. So it is here. God himself intervened in this tragic account of failure with grace that seeks to bring redemption.

We see this grace in several places. John Wesley suggested that the question "Where art thou?" should be looked on as a gracious pursuit designed to recover Adam and Eve.[13] This image of God shows him as a seeking, initiating God. Scantily covered and cringing in shame and fear, Adam and Eve attempt to hide from God. They have spurned grace and have become strangers to it. They avoid any contact with God and have no strength to initiate their own redemption. They can find redemption only through a God who initiates and seeks fallen humanity. Thankfully, that's the nature of God. He constantly seeks and initiates redemption for fallen creatures. He finds us at the bottom, stuck in the slough of despond, and picks us up.

[margin handwriting: God is an initiator, especially for redemption for His fallen creatures]

[margin handwriting: "You are okay, I have you"]

This picture of the seeking God of grace is evident in the poem *The Hound of Heaven*. Francis Thompson saw God as an unhurried presence pursuing him through life, seeking to redeem him. While God seeks, Thompson flees. The first verse captures these two images: humanity's avoidance of God and the God who continually seeks.

[margin handwriting: But maybe slow, but God endured our running]

> I fled Him, down the nights and down the days;
>   I fled Him, down the arches of the years:
> I fled Him, down the labyrinthine ways
>   Of my own mind; and in the mist of tears
> I hid from Him, and under running laughter.
>   Up vistaed hopes I sped;
>   And shot, precipitated,
> Adown Titanic glooms of chasmed fears,
>   From those strong Feet that followed, followed after.
>   But with unhurrying chase,
>   And unperturbèd pace,
> Deliberate speed, majestic instancy,
>   They beat—and a Voice beat
>   More instant than the Feet—
> "All things betray thee, who betrayest Me."[14]

What inspires this relentless pursuit? Thompson indicated grace was the source. In the final verse, he captured this theme. The pursuit springs from God's unmerited love of one who is "little worthy of any love . . . ." For Thompson, God is one who makes much of that which is worthy of nothing. The poet's intent is clear: God's relentless pursuit of sinful humanity springs from his unmerited love of humanity.

Thompson gave another reason for God's pursuit of grace: He does not pursue us to rob us or harm us. Rather, he desires that we receive all of life's goods as gifts from his hand. Once we surrender to the divine pursuer, we discover that what we had thought we lost has been stored for us. Thus Thompson wrote:

> "All which I took from thee I did but take,
>   Not for thy harms,
> But just that thou might'st seek it in My arms.
>   All which thy child's mistake
> Fancies as lost, I have stored for thee at home:
>   Rise, clasp My hand, and come!"[15]

Grace in Confession

We can also discern grace it in the question of Genesis 3:13: "What is this that you have done?" In an earlier chapter, I suggested that Adam and Eve took shame's route. That is, they chose to cover up their deeds rather than come clean. God's question called them to squarely own and confess their sin. It's the kind of query that could lead them to appropriate guilt and thus get them back on the road to redemption.

For many persons confession seems like a low moment. It represents a humbling before others, certainly not something in which one could find any grace. Therefore, we often avoid confession. Commentator Adam Clarke lamented this human tendency:

> How few ingenuously confess their own sin! They see not their guilt. They are continually making excuses

for their crimes; the strength and subtlety of the
tempter, the natural weakness of their own minds, the
unfavorable circumstances in which they were placed,
etc., etc., are all pleaded as excuses for their sins, and
thus the possibility of repentance is precluded; for till
a man take his sin to himself, till he acknowledge that
he alone is guilty, he cannot be humbled, and conse-
quently cannot be saved.[16]

Rather than being a low moment, confession is a high
moment. Oscar Wilde apparently understood this para-
doxical aspect of confession. In a letter sent from prison,
Wilde is reputed to have written: "A man's very highest
moment is, I have no doubt at all, when he kneels in the
dust, and beats his breast, and tells all the sins of his
life."[17] If that confession is made to God, it's a high moment indeed. Confession clears violated consciences. It
throws open the doors of God's grace to poor impoverished souls. It sets us back on the road to responsible
living. It begins to work its transforming power in our
lives. In fact, confession is the doorway to healing of
every kind. We never experience renewal of health and
restoration without it.

Grace in Consequences

Sin always brings its consequences. One consequence is
becoming culpable for our deeds. In the Genesis narrative, we saw some of these emotional consequences expressed as shame and fear. But other consequences are
clearly evidenced in Genesis 3:14–19. All the participants
in this monumental failure experience consequences. For
example, the serpent is cursed and doomed to crawl on
his belly, among other things. Graciously, the human
couple are not cursed but they, too, would suffer. But even
here a strange grace holds us responsible for our deeds.
It will not free us from the consequences of our deeds.

To some, an insistence on consequences is the very opposite of grace. To them, real grace would totally set the person free without consequences. However, that's not true grace; it's myopic, nearsighted grace that doesn't see the long view. True grace is not only interested in our present, it's also interested in preserving our future. One cannot preserve another's future if one negates consequences of wrong actions. Sinners who do not experience consequences may believe that sin is all right and will fall into greater sins. To free them from bondage to sin, one must establish and enforce consequences.

Grace—A Promise of God's Goodwill

Grace does for us what we cannot do for ourselves. Grace redeems and restores us. We saw such intent in the image of the seeking God who searches us out. We also saw it in the push to bring the wayward couple to confession. Some also see redemption in two other images drawn from the Fall narrative. The first instance is found in Genesis 3:15. This has been called the *Protevangelium* because some see in it a prototype of the Christian gospel. In the words about the woman's offspring who will bruise the serpent's head, many see an image of Jesus and the promise of his redemption. For those persons, the destroying of the serpent's head points to the destruction of the devil's power and lordship over humankind. They suggest that in this act, Christ redeems us and returns us to God.[18] Some also see the image of redemption in Genesis 3:21 where God clothes the couple. He covers their inadequate efforts with a more adequate covering, clothing made from the skins of slain animals. Some see in the shedding of animals' blood a sacrifice made for the forgiveness of sins.

Even if one disagrees with a salvation interpretation of these verses, one should not miss God's significant activity on the couple's behalf. God clothed this couple. He sought to protect them from continued shame and embarrassment by providing them more adequate garments. Because they were driven from the well-regulated garden into a harsh world, God would not let them go out fully unprotected, so he clothed them. In this act we see God as a preserver and as one who offers them his abiding goodwill.[19] That goodwill would eventually lead to the ultimate act of grace—the sending and dying of the Son of God to redeem us.

Grace Is Not Cheap

Grace is abundantly available, but we must always remember that it is never cheap. It abounds where sin abounds but it is costly. Grace cost the Son of God his life. It was grace purchased at a high price. Once we experience grace, it also makes demands of us. Rightly understood, grace calls us to responsibility. It demands a positive response to God. We dare not receive it in vain. Grace by its very nature is transforming. Anything that does not produce this transformation and its accompanying fruits of righteousness is "cheap grace."

In *The Cost of Discipleship*, Dietrich Bonhoeffer gives this description of cheap grace:

> Cheap grace means grace sold on the market like cheapjack's wares. The sacraments, the forgiveness of sin, and the consolations of religion are thrown away at cut prices. Grace is represented as the Church's inexhaustible treasury, from which she showers blessings with generous hands, without asking questions or fixing limits . . . Grace alone does everything, they say, and so everything can remain as it was before.[20]

In a later section Bonhoeffer continued his description of cheap grace:

Cheap grace is the preaching of forgiveness without requiring repentance, baptism without Church discipline, Communion without confession, absolution without contrition. Cheap grace is grace without discipleship, grace without the cross, grace without Jesus Christ, living and incarnate.[21]

In short, cheap grace is irresponsible grace. It requires nothing of us. We can profess to possess it but yet remain the same. This is not true grace but a deceiving sham. It is worlds apart from true grace which calls us to a new way of living and being. True grace begins its transforming work *within* persons, but inevitably it shows itself *without* in righteous conduct.

Nothing else is worthy of the name grace. Oswald Chambers, in his classic devotional book *My Utmost for His Highest*, says: "We have to develop godly habits to express what God's grace has done in us. It is not just a question of being saved from hell, but of being saved so that 'the life of Jesus may also be manifested in our body.'"[22] Grace calls us to live responsibly and ultimately to be fashioned into the very image of Christ.

Endnotes

1. Randy L. Maddox, *Responsible Grace* (Nashville: Kingswood Books, 1994), p. 87.
2. Ibid.
3. Matthew Henry, *Commentary on the Whole Bible: Condensed Version* (Albany, Ore.: Ages Software, Version 2.0, 1997), p. 14.
4. Maddox, op. cit., p. 86.
5. Ibid.
6. H. Richard Niebuhr, *The Responsible Self* (New York: Harper and Row), 1963.
7. Dietrich Bonhoeffer, *The Cost of Discipleship*, trans. R. H. Fuller (London: SCM Press, 1948), p. 192.
8. Ibid.
9. Gerhard Von Rad, *Genesis* (Philadelphia: Westminster Press, 1972), p. 89.

10. Quoted in Adam Clarke, *Clarke's Commentary, Volume 1: Genesis–Deuteronomy* (Albany, Ore.: Ages Software, Version 2.0, 1997), p. 59.

11. Adam Clarke, *Clarke's Commentary, Volume 1: Genesis–Deuteronomy* (Albany, Ore.: Ages Software, Version 2.0, 1997), p. 44.

12. H. Richard Niebuhr, *The Responsible Self* (New York: Harper and Row, 1963), p. 52.

13. John Wesley, *Commentary on Genesis* (Albany Ore.: Ages software, Version 2.0, 1997), p. 35.

14. Francis Thompson, *The Hound of Heaven*, Published 1893.

15. Ibid.

16. Adam Clarke, op. cit. p. 62.

17. Oscar Wilde in a letter to Lord Alfred Douglas following Wilde's trial and imprisonment, written in prison, accessed from Microsoft Bookshelf, 2000.

18. Commentators Adam Clarke and Matthew Henry see this possibility. There appears to be a long line of Christian tradition that interprets this passage in that light. Others like Gerhard Von Rad would disagree with this position.

19. See Gerhard Von Rad, *Genesis* (Philadelphia: Westminster, 1972) and Kenneth A. Matthews, *Genesis 1–11:26*, Volume 1A (Nashville: Broadman and Holman, 1996). Both see the act of clothing as having marked significance.

20. Dietrich Bonhoeffer, *The Cost of Discipleship*, trans. R. H. Fuller (London: SCM Press, 1948), p. 37.

21. Ibid., p. 38.

22. Oswald Chambers, *My Utmost for His Highest* (Grand Rapids: Discovery House, 1992), devotional reading for May 14.

Questions for Further Study

1. Do you agree with the author that God's boundaries and limits on human freedom are part of his grace? Why or why not?

2. How would we experience God's grace if we did not sin? Could we experience it?

3. Was the term "prevenient grace" new to you? Describe examples of its working in your life to bring you to God.

4. The author writes: "[Grace] enables us to respond [to God] but never coerces our response." Why doesn't

God overpower our will so that we choose his good and joyful course in our lives?

5. How is living responsibly in our relationship with creation intertwined with our call to live responsibly in our relationship with other human beings?

6. How do you respond graciously to yourself, as the author says we must if we are to mimic God's grace, without sliding into self-centeredness?

7. List several examples of practical ways we can extend God's grace to other persons.

8. Many people today contend that human beings are simply more highly evolved animals and not a special creation. How does the Genesis creation narrative refute that popular contemporary belief?

9. Do you agree with the author that the idea of absolute freedom without any boundaries or limits is a myth? Explain your answer.

10. How can God's graciously devised boundaries promote self-discovery?

11. Why is confession a necessary part of spiritual healing and restoration?

12. Why is it necessary for us to experience the consequences of our sin, even after we have been forgiven? What would happen if God made sin's negative consequences disappear after we confess our sin?

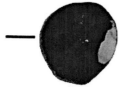

Bibliography

Aalders, G. *Genesis* (Grand Rapids: Regency Reference Library, Zondervan Publishing House, 1981).

Albers, R. H. *Shame: A Faith Perspective* (New York: The Haworth Pastoral Press, 1995).

Anderson, Ray. *Self Care* (Wheaton Ill.: Victor Books, 1995).

Ball-Kilbourne, Gary L. *Get Acquainted with Your Bible* (Nashville, Tenn.: Abingdon, 1993).

Becket, Samuel. *Waiting for Godot: Tragicomedy in 2 Acts*, Act 1, (New York: Grove Press, 1954).

Berecz, John. M., and Herbert. W. Helm, Jr. "Shame: The Underside of Christianity." *Journal of Psychology and Christianity*, 1998, Vol. 17:1, 5–14.

Bonhoeffer, Dietrich. *Creation and Fall: A Theological Exposition of Genesis 1–3*, trans. D. S. Bax (Minneapolis, Minn.: Fortress Press, 1997).

Bonhoeffer, Dietrich. *Life Together*, trans. John W. Doberstein (New York: Harper and Row, 1954).

Bonhoeffer, Dietrich. *The Cost of Discipleship*, trans. R. H. Fuller (London: SCM Press, 1948).

Bonhoeffer, Dietrich. "The Structure of Responsible Life," in James M. Gustafson and James T. Laney, eds., *On Being Responsible; Issues in Personal Ethics* (New York: Harper and Row, 1968).

Bradshaw, John. *Healing the Shame that Binds You* (Audiocassette) (Florida: Health Communications, 1989).

Branden, Nathaniel. *Taking Responsibility* (New York: Fireside, 1996).

Brown, William. *Character in Crisis* (Grand Rapids: William B. Eerdmans, 1996).

Bunyan, John. *Bunyan's Life or Grace Abounding to the Chief of Sinners* (Albany, Ore.: Ages Software, Version 2.0, 1996, 1997).

Chambers, Oswald. *My Utmost for His Highest* (Grand Rapids: Discovery House, 1992).

Clarke, Adam. *Commentary on Genesis* (Albany, Ore.: Ages Software, Version 2.0, 1996, 1997).

Cloud, Henry, and John Townsend. *Boundaries* (Grand Rapids: Zondervan, 1992).

Collins, Kenneth J. *Soul Care: Deliverance and Renewal Through the Christian Life* (Wheaton, Ill.: Victor Books, 1995).

Fossom, M., and M. Mason. *Facing Shame: Families in Recovery.* (New York: W. W. Norton, 1986).

Glasser, William. *Choice Theory* (New York: HarperCollins, 1998).

Glasser, William. *Reality Therapy: A New Approach to Psychiatry* (New York: Harper and Row, 1965).

Goleman, Daniel. *Emotional Intelligence* (New York: Bantam Books, 1995).

Gustafson, James M., and James T. Laney. "Introduction," in James M. Gustafson and James T. Laney, eds., *On Being Responsible* (New York: Harper and Row, 1968).

Hanford, Thomas, ed. *2010 Popular Quotations* (Albany, Ore.: Ages Software, Version 2.0, 1997).

Hardy, Lee. *The Fabric of this World* (Grand Rapids: Eerdmans Publishing Company, 1990).

Harper, James M., and Margaret H. Hoopes. *Uncovering Shame* (New York: W. W. Norton, 1990).

Haring, Bernard. "Essential Concepts of Moral Theology," in James M. Gustafson and James T. Laney, eds., *On Being Responsible* (New York: Harper and Row, 1968).

Harris, Sydney J. *On the Contrary* (Cambridge, Mass.: Riverside Press, 1962).

Harris, R. Laird, and Gleason L. Archer, and Bruce K. Waltke, *Theological Wordbook of the Old Testament* (Chicago: Moody Press, 1981).

Henry, Matthew. *Commentary on the Whole Bible: Condensed Version* (Albany, Ore.: Ages Software, Version 2.0, 1997).

Hawthorne, Nathaniel. *The Scarlet Letter* (New York: Alfred A. Knopf, 1992).

Jenkins, Frank M. III. "A Thin Excuse for Obesity," *Lexington Herald-Leader*, November 29, 1996.

Jones, Judy. "Father by Default," *Lexington Herald-Leader*, November 1, 1997.

Juipe, Dean. "Tyson Talks About Holyfield Bout," *Las Vegas Sun*, November 4, 1997.

Lasseter, Tom. "First-Grade Teacher at Cassidy Is Charged with Prostitution," *Lexington Herald-Leader*, February 15, 2000.

Lewis, C. S. *A Grief Observed* (New York: The Seabury Press, 1963).

Lewis, Michael. *Shame: The Exposed Self* (New York: The Free Press, 1992).

Lexington Herald-Leader, "Many Call Judge in Au Pair Case Too Lenient," November 12, 1997.

Lynd, Helen M. *On Shame and the Search for Identity* (New York: Harcourt, Brace and Company, 1958).

Maddox, Randy L. *Responsible Grace* (Nashville: Kingswood Books, 1994).

Madigan, Tim, and John Gonzalez, and Potter. "Gunman Hated Mother, Women—and Himself," *Lexington Herald-Leader*, October 22, 1991.

Mandeville, Bernard. *The Fable of the Bees* (1714; rev. 1723). Quoted in *The Columbia Dictionary of Quotations*, Columbia University Press, 1993, 1995, 1997, 1998 in *Microsoft Bookshelf®* 1987–1999, Microsoft Corp.

Marin, Peter. "Living in Moral Pain," *Psychology Today*, November 1981, pp. 68–80.

Mascall, E. L. *The Importance of Being Human* (Westport, Conn.: Greenwood Press, 1958).

Matthews, K. *New American Commentary: Genesis*, Vol. 1A (Nashville, Tenn.: Broadman and Holman, 1996).

Menninger, Karl. *Whatever Became of Sin* (New York: Hawthorne Books, 1974).

Niebuhr, H. Richard. "The Meaning of Responsibility," in James M. Gustafson and James T. Laney, eds., *On Being Responsible* (New York: Harper and Row, 1968).

Niebuhr, H. Richard. *The Responsible Self* (New York: Harper and Row, 1963).

Page, Clarence. "What Help Do We Owe Others?" *Lexington Herald-Leader*, September 2, 1998.

Pine-Coffin, R. S. (trans.), *Saint Augustine Confessions* (Baltimore: Penguin Books, 1961).

Satir, Virginia. *The New People Making* (Mountain View, Calif.: Science and Behavior Books, 1988).

Schlessinger, Laura. *10 Stupid Things Couples Do to Mess Up Their Relationships* (New York: Cliff Street Books, 2001).

Schlossberger, Eugene. *Moral Responsibility and Persons* (Philadelphia: Temple University Press, 1992).

Schoeman, Ferdinand. *Responsibility, Character and Emotions* (New York: Cambridge University Press, 1987).

Shakespeare, William. *The Complete Works of Shakespeare: King John* (New York: Doubleday and Company, 1936).

Shepherd, Chuck. "News of the Weird: Blame the Police," *Lexington Herald-Leader*, November 7, 1997.

Shepherd, Chuck. "News of the Weird: Crazy Accusation," *Lexington Herald-Leader*, November 7, 1997.

Swinburne, Richard. *Responsibility and Atonement* (Oxford: Clarendon Press, 1989).

Tangney. June, P. "Shame and Guilt in Interpersonal Relationships," in June P. Tangney and Kurt W. Fischer, eds., *Self-Conscious Emotions* (New York: The Guilford Press, 1995).

Tangney, June P., and Susan A. Burggraf, and Patricia E. Wagner. "Shame-Proneness, Guilt-Proneness and Psychological Symptoms," in June P. Tangney and Kurt W. Fischer, eds., *Self-Conscious Emotions* (New York: The Guilford Press, 1995).

Thompson, Francis. "The Hound of Heaven" (1893).

Von Rad, Gerhard. *Genesis* (Philadelphia: Westminster Press, 1972).

Webster, Sarah A. "What Happened to Jamil," *Lexington Herald-Leader*, January 11, 1998.

Wesley, John. *Commentary on Genesis* (Albany Ore.: Ages Software, Version 2.0, 1997).

Wilde, Oscar. *The Picture of Dorian Gray* (London: Unicorn Press, 1945).

Worthington, Everett L. *Marriage Counseling* (Downers Grove, Ill.: InterVarsity Press, 1989).

Lightning Source UK Ltd.
Milton Keynes UK
UKOW03f0903061216
289286UK00002B/441/P

9 781609 470944